YOUR FIRST
MOTORCYCLE

YOUR FIRST MOTORCYCLE

BE SAFE, START RIGHT, AND HAVE FUN

LEE HEAVER

LIONCREST

PUBLISHING

YOUR FIRST MOTORCYCLE

Be Safe, Start Right, and Have Fun

ISBN 978-1-61961-778-0 *Paperback*

978-1-61961-777-3 *Ebook*

CONTENTS

FOREWORD

I first met Lee Heaver three years ago during my quest to become a motorcycle rider. Being a safety-oriented individual, I wanted the reassurance that came with becoming a graduate of 1st Gear Motorcycle School. Not only did the school offer much needed ride time in a safe environment, it also taught the skills necessary to pass the Motorcycle Skills Test. Lee's demeanor and ability to communicate important information in a fun but altruistic way helped the process enormously. Clearly, Lee is a person who loves motorcycles and the associated lifestyle; his authentic love for the sport instantly rubs off on any student. There's enthusiasm with Lee, but there's also an intense emphasis on safety. It's like he feels responsible for each and every one of his students' well-being, which is a very good thing considering he's teaching you to perform on an inherently risky mode of transportation.

Lee's book, *Your First Motorcycle*, is exactly like the man him-self: easy to read, full of stories, and basic enough for anyone to understand. I jest, but more seriously, Lee's conversational authorship makes it both incredibly easy to read and hugely informative. Tackling all the necessary information anyone interested in becoming a motorcycle rider or who is still in the novice to intermediate stages would need, the book offers practical tips on how to tell your loved ones you're taking up a dangerous hobby, to how to score deals on your first set of leathers (riding gear) and what to look for when purchasing your first motorcycle. In a sense, I feel like Lee has compiled all the behind-the-scenes conversations and frequently asked questions from every student he has ever put through 1st Gear's program in this new understandable support guide. Likely, this book will fit in your insurance pouch under the seat and should probably stay there for your first season or two of riding.

GEOFFREY THOR DESMOULIN, PHD, RKIN

Formerly the engineering host on the hit television show, Deadliest Warrior, Geoffrey is now President of GTD Engineering Inc., a forensic engineering company. When he's not consulting on injury biomechanics, incident reconstruction, and physical testing, Geoffrey can be found riding his motorcycle in his hometown of Vancouver and beyond.

INTRODUCTION

I remember my maiden motorcycle ride, every last minute of those six hours from my hometown of Vancouver, British Columbia, to Kamloops ski resort in the region's interior. It was summer and I'd never taken my motorcycle past city limits. That day, it was just me, my bike, and my riding buddy. I had nothing to worry about except the road in front of me, keeping the speed reasonable and safe, and taking in the warm, rich smells and sights around me.

It was a new and truly immersive way to travel. I was in the landscape, not just riding by it. I became aware of how much of the world there was to explore and experience. When you're in a car, you always want to take the quickest route, but on a motorcycle, I discovered you're intent on finding the more interesting and twisty one. Riding my bike, I felt free, challenged, and aware of how rewarding riding could be. That day, motorcycles became my passion.

Growing up, I'd had a general interest in motorcycles. My dad rode one for a bit, but it wasn't until I started looking at sport bikes that I thought how cool they were. That's when my interest in motorcycles was cemented. The thing was, as much as I admired the people who rode them, and wished that I could ride one myself, I was too timid to try. It wasn't until 2005 that my wish became realized, when the girl I was dating introduced me to a guy who rode motorcycles. His brother owned a motorcycle school, and I signed up, took the course, and bought my first bike for $2,900—a 1989 Honda CB1—and got a full license. The following year, I found myself on that unforgettable ride to Kamloops.

MOTORCYCLE CULTURE

After Kamloops, I went on ride after ride, always choosing to take the interesting roads, the ones that inevitably led to even more interesting things and people. Many of the people I would meet were also into motorcycle riding. In fact, I made a completely new circle of friends. It felt as if I'd joined this special new club and, in many ways, I had. After all, you had to have a motorcycle and be able to ride it safely to be a part of it. While that sounds exclusive, in meeting this new, like-minded group of people, I felt included; I felt I belonged.

Never was this more true than during a group ride I organized from Vancouver down the rolling coast to Oregon in the Pacific Northwest region of the United States. I can spend hours crafting routes to ride and names for them. This one I called ExplOregon. While we all left Vancouver together, for most of the eight days we were traveling, we all took different roads. Connected by Sena, a Bluetooth communication device attached to our helmets, we chatted while we rode. We warned each other about gravel on the road, a big rock, a piece of wood, an animal, an oncoming police car, or if we needed to stop for gas, a snack, or to rest.

The chatting didn't end on the roadway. At night, we'd catch up over dinner and drinks, exchanging stories. We'd talk about everything—the twisty roads, how our motorcycles rode upon them, if our bikes needed fixing along the way, the random places where we ate lunch, what motorcycles we were going to buy next, the modifications we were going to make to our bikes, and of course, after a while, our family lives. It's strange. We were twenty-four people of different ages, sexes, and personalities, but this ride taught me there's nothing like sharing a dangerous activity to open you to a rare kind of camaraderie.

And that's it. That's what's so great about motorcycle culture. Anyone can be a part of it. There's no typical motorcyclist. I've met and connected with people from twenty-five to sixty-three years old—parents with younger kids, parents whose kids have grown up and now they're getting into riding, students who own a bike to keep down the expense of commuting and parking, the occasional person who just wants to take the motorcycle out on a Sunday for an hour, and individuals who live and breathe motorcycles (like me).

THE REAL DIFFICULTIES AND DANGERS OF MOTORCYCLE RIDING

Whatever their level of interest, age, or circumstances, motorcycle riders definitely have one big thing in common, other than a love for bikes (no, I don't mean they are outlaws or dangerous people who make poor life choices, have tattoos, are convicted felons, or are compulsory brawlers—contrary to what public opinion may say). What riders have in common is a healthy awareness of the very real difficulties and dangers of motorcycle riding.

The dangers involved in motorcycle riding begin with taking your learner's license test. A multiple-choice quiz taken at your nearest motor vehicle licensing agency is tough to fail. While that sounds like a good thing, it's foolhardy to think you're well equipped after passing it to jump on a bike and get riding. You're not—in fact, you couldn't be further from it.

If you're like every other eager, yet inexperienced rider I've met, you'll still charge off to buy a bike. You'll fall in love with an expensive, inappropriately big motorcycle or possibly a cheap, unreliable one. Either way, the chance of you ending up with a bike you can't ride is high. That motorcycle, which in the moment seemed like such a good idea, is going to cost you time and cash to sell or fix. What you now have is a problem: a motorcycle that's unrideable, and you haven't even left the garage.

Should you manage to hop on your motorcycle, your next challenge will be balance. Motorcycles fall over easily and driving them takes a smoothness, a steadiness that's not easily learned. A motorcycle will not stop instantly. In a car, you can just hammer on the brakes and let the ABS take care of it, but with a motorcycle, you have to think about stopping ahead of time and applying the brakes slowly and with ease.

You will need to apply those brakes often while riding. When you start riding your motorcycle, you're going to feel you're flying down the road even though you may be the slowest vehicle on it. This is your self-preservation talking and encouraging you to keep your speed low, but as soon as you gain confidence, you'll lose any last sense you have of your speed. You'll think you're still within the speed limit. But trust me. You'll be exceeding it and may now be the most dangerous thing on the road.

The police and motorcyclists might see you tearing along, but other vehicles on the road definitely won't, and that's another issue. As a motorcyclist, you're one very exposed rider in what is a car and truck world. You could have the loudest motorcycle exhaust pipes and be wearing the brightest of colors, but if you ride around thinking everyone can see you, at best, you're going to be disappointed by car and truck drivers. At worst, everything you take for granted could be destroyed if you collide with one.

FROM RIDING TO TEACHING TO WRITING

By now, I hope it's dawning on you that you can't just climb on a motorcycle and figure it out. That would be akin to learning how to drive in a Lamborghini. Even the cheapest motorcycles perform like expensive sports cars. Trust me. You are not prepared for that kind of power and performance. Somebody has to be there, whether it's your Uncle Bob or an actual professional instructor, because there is too much for you to learn and master on your own. Wanting to learn things the right way, I went the professional instructor route. In 2014, I gave up my desk job as a financial planner to become an instructor. Motorcycling being the tight-knit community that it is, naturally I stayed in touch with the guy who first introduced me to riding. I later partnered with him to open 1st Gear Motorcycle School in Vancouver, BC, Canada. Now, I get to be outside most of the time, in all types of weather, sharing my enthusiasm and love for motorcycle riding with people just as enthusiastic to learn how to ride.

Over the twelve years I've been riding and teaching others to ride, I've learned that when you're on a motorcycle, it's always a balancing act between enjoying it and being awake to the bad things that can happen to you or others. Helping you navigate that balance is what this book is all about. In the chapters to come, I'm going to show you the best, safest, and most cost-effective ways to get into motorcycle riding. It's my greatest wish that by reading this book, you won't have to crash your way to becoming a good motorcyclist.

CHAPTER 1

COMPLETING THE PAPERWORK AND TELLING FRIENDS AND FAMILY

When I learned how to scuba dive, my parents pointed out all the dangers with it. They didn't see what I saw: while scuba diving is potentially dangerous, it's the safest high-risk activity out there. As dangerous activities go, scuba diving is far safer than motorcycle riding. You can imagine, then, that when it came to telling my parents I wanted to learn how to ride a motorcycle, I was hesitant. I was so hesitant, in fact, that I didn't tell them straight away. I decided to get my learner's license, go through a safety course, buy a bike and protective gear and then tell them. I figured this was the best way to communicate my intention to ride safely and seriously.

When I did get around to telling my family, the news of my new hobby was met with long silences. To say they were disappointed is an understatement and yet, when they saw me on my motorcycle, that disappointment turned to mild interest, but only mild. They still weren't thrilled about the whole idea. Even today, if I were to tell my parents I was getting out of motorcycles, they'd probably be overjoyed about it. Given that motorcycles can bring an immense amount of happiness, the prospect of being forbidden to ride them by family or regulating authorities makes this chapter an important one for you to start with. Clearing your decision to ride a motorcycle with the people in your life who matter will definitely save you a hassle in the long run. Besides, you wouldn't want them finding out about your new passion after a crash lands you in the emergency room.

HOW TO GET A MOTORCYCLE LEARNER'S LICENSE

You may or may not want to begin by telling your family,

but you will definitely want to tell the regulating authority. It's through the authority—namely, your local department of motor vehicles (DMV)—that you'll need to apply for your motorcycle learner's license. The minimum age to drive a motorcycle varies from country to country and state to state, but in most places, you can apply for a motorcycle license at the same age at which you qualify to drive a car.

Depending on where you live, you may have to pass a written exam before you can get your learner's license. The exam, taken at the DMV's physical location, will test your knowledge of motorcycle safety, traffic rules, and regulations. To prepare for the exam, you'll want to download the motorcycle operator's manual (or something similar, again depending upon where you live) from your local DMV website and study it. Don't overthink studying and taking the written test. If you can fog a mirror with your breath, you'll probably pass. If you're already a driver, one to two hours of study should take care of this simple, multiple-choice test. To be extra sure you'll pass, though, you might also want to take some online sample tests.

Before taking your test, you'll also need to check with your local DMV office about what kind of documentation you'll need to bring along with you (e.g., birth certificate, identification card, etc.), and whether or not fees are involved. At the time of your learner's license test, you may also have to pass a vision exam. Again, this depends on where you live.

While it may sound as if there are many variables in this process, the hardest part of it will be the effort involved in physically going to the licensing office, waiting around to take your test, and the usual hardships involved in dealing with government bureaucrats. That said, don't in any way be tempted to skip this process. The learner's license is necessary for whoever you are and wherever you live. Without one, you won't be legally permitted to operate a motorcycle.

At the same time as being aware of what's minimally expected of you with a learner's license, be sure to check with your local DMV for what's not permitted. Typically, learners are not permitted to drive their motorcycle at night or on the freeway. Carrying passengers on the back of your bike is also—and rightly so—a no-no.

Your motorcycle learner's license is usually valid for up to one year, within which time you're expected to learn how to safely ride a motorcycle and prepare for and take your final and full motorcycle license exam. The final exam involves an examiner watching you ride your motorcycle. The nature of the exam varies everywhere. In California, it's a quick parking lot test, but here in British Columbia, the examiner watches you ride your motorcycle through the city for a full thirty minutes. Please don't rush into your final road test. Consider it a concert performance. You'd never learn the piano or guitar for a measly ten hours and then play in front of thousands of fans. They'd boo you off the stage! It's the very same with motorcycle riding, so be sure you have the confidence, comfort, and a good understanding of the road rules.

HOW TO TELL YOUR FRIENDS AND FAMILY

While most people don't allow us to tell them that their bad eating habits are affecting their health, you won't find the same reserve when it comes to advice on motorcycles. People will always tell you motorcycling is dangerous. Indeed, they'll tell you to your face that you're going to crash and get hurt. Their concern is, ordinarily, founded on some story they were told about a neighbor, cousin, or dog walker's friend who broke an arm or lost an arm or worse while riding a motorcycle. That one motorcycle crash story has fused in their mind the idea that death befalls anyone who rides one.

Certainly, I don't want to make light of the dangers of riding motorcycles, but I do want to highlight that the odds of your loved ones supporting your new hobby are stacked against you. Your task, therefore, is not to convince them they're wrong; it's to help them understand what you're going to do to make motorcycle riding as safe as it can be.

When I got around to telling my parents about riding a motorcycle, I told them while wearing head-to-toe motor-cycle gear. It was not for dramatic effect that I chose this approach—although, trust me, you will feel and look good in it—but more to emphasize that I was fully aware of the dangers of riding and that by wearing protective gear, I was consciously minimizing the risk. You may want to do the same. You may also want to tell your family that you plan to take a motorcycle safety course and that you're going to start on a small motorcycle to just see what it's all about. Of course, if you're truly afraid of what your parents may think, and you know they're going to forbid you to ride one as long as you live under their roof, you may not want to tell them at all.

Not telling your wife or significant other, however, will likely be out of the question. My advice here is to persuade that person, over time, with the same safety-first plan: you'll wear protective gear, take a motorcycle safety course, and buy a small bike. If they say no, ask again six months later, or a year later, and then every year after that. Eventually, they may relent. Equally, they may threaten to leave you if you ever get on a motorcycle. Over time, you will have the chance to figure out whether motorcycle riding is worth the risk of losing your partner.

FOREST FIRES AND BLAZES OF DISAPPROVAL

When you take your bike off the main highways, you're seeking the quietest, most picturesque roads. One summer, on a group ride through the quiet roads of Montana, we were coming down a steep mountain pass when we saw a column of smoke. Nearing the smoke, we could see a small fire, presumably the result of someone thoughtlessly throwing away a cigarette butt. It was expanding with every minute that passed, and as nobody else was in the vicinity, we hopped off our bikes and started kicking dirt and throwing whatever liquids we had over it. The only thing we didn't throw on that fire was the bottle of gin we had left over from the night before. The fire had started long before we arrived; yet, no one had stopped to help extinguish it. We were the only ones who'd pulled over to put the fire out. Eventually, other motorists did see the effort we were putting in and soon we had help. A passing RV offered up a fire extinguisher and extra water, and finally, we started winning. The fire stopped spreading and by the time the fire department showed up, they had little work to do and were very thankful.

This is just one of many motorcycle adventure stories I have. Such adventures await you. In this story of a Montana forest fire, there's also a cautionary tale, however. Do not carelessly throw yourself on a bike without first seeking the right permissions. As casual littering can be serious, so can riding. Be thoughtful, and you will never have to put out blazes of disapproval.

CHAPTER 2

CHOOSING THE RIGHT TRAINING PROGRAM

Back in the day, your Uncle Bob taught you how to ride a motorcycle on a Sunday afternoon. If you consider how qualified your Uncle Bob was to teach you, you'll rightly conclude that he was more or less leaving you to figure motorcycling out along the way. It's no surprise, then, that back in the late 1970s and early 1980s, if you were a motorcyclist, thirty years of age or younger, you had an 80 percent chance of dying on your beloved bike. While those odds have come down in recent years, they're still not great for new riders.

To ensure against meeting your end on a bike, it's critical to remember that when it comes to riding a motorcycle, you are the most important safety feature. To make certain that safety feature is top notch, I can't recommend motorcycle safety training enough. Yes, you could learn to ride a motorcycle on your own and for many, it can be easy. After all, if you can ride a bicycle with a small commitment on your behalf, you can learn how to properly ride a motorcycle. What's difficult, however, is staying safe. Motorcycle training courses make you practice safety maneuvers repeatedly. It's that repetition and attention to detail that will save your life.

Make no mistake, getting some solid motorcycle training under your helmet will cost you time and money, but it will save you in the long run. For starters, you get to learn on someone else's motorcycle, so if you make mistakes (and you will), it's not your own motorcycle you're beating up. For those still on the fence about riding, taking a course is an inexpensive way to try motorcycles out without making the full investment in a bike and gear, not to mention maintenance and insurance. Finally, and more meaningfully, if taking this course stops you from making one bad decision on the bike that could be fatal, then it's done more than save your wallet; it's saved your life.

WHAT IS A MOTORCYCLE TRAINING PROGRAM AND WHAT DO THEY TEACH?

Motorcycle safety training teaches both new and experienced riders how to handle their bike on the open road safely and confidently. While laws requiring motorcycle safety training vary from country to country and state to state, the safe-riding knowledge and experience a rider can gain from them is invaluable.

Motorcycle safety schools can be privately run, nonprofit, or government-owned. Courses may vary in terms of time (typically, they run between sixteen and thirty hours), but they shouldn't vary in terms of what they teach. Instruction should be divided between a classroom and practical parking lot experience, ideally including:

Classroom

- Licensing process
- Insuring your motorcycle
- Motorcycle risks and hazards and how to beat them
- Motorcycle gear and why you should wear it
- Motorcycle parts and controls
- Gears and braking
- Cornering and body positioning
- Lane positioning and spacing
- Motorcycle tires
- How to handle intersections and highways

- Riding in the rain and wind
- How to ride with passengers
- How to pass your road test
- Basic motorcycle maintenance

Parking Lot

- Checking over your motorcycle for safety
- How to mount and dismount a motorcycle
- Proper posture on your bike
- Starting the motorcycle
- The throttle and controls
- Slow speed maneuvering
- Shifting gears
- Cornering
- Counter steering and swerving
- Emergency braking
- Testing

WHAT TO LOOK FOR IN A TRAINING PROGRAM

The ratio of classroom to parking lot time is a great initial indicator of quality training. Ideally, you're looking for a course that offers a minimum of six hours on the lot. This should give you plenty of time to repeat and practice maneuvers under the watchful eye of a (hopefully) well-qualified instructor. The lot, incidentally, should be a decent size—the bigger, the better. On a big lot, you'll be able to ride around at speeds closely related to some of the speeds you will do on the road. If you learn on a training lot the size of a postage stamp, you'll be forced to roam around at ten miles/ fifteen kilometers an hour. When you go for your first road rides, the speeds on the road are going to be much higher, so your learning curve will be mighty steep.

Speaking of steep, don't draw the false conclusion that an expensive course is necessarily a good course. A motorcycle course can cost as little as $200 and as much as $1,000. The cost of the course has more to do with the costs of operating a motorcycle school in a particular location and is no indicator of the value it's going to bring you.

Don't make money the deciding factor when choosing a training program, but do make the reputation of the instructors a consideration. Be sure to check the instructors' page on the motorcycle safety school's website and verify their accreditation, if any. You may also want to look at the school's reviews. Just because someone is an excellent motorcycle rider doesn't necessarily mean that person can teach. I'd recommend finding a school that has two, three, or even four motorcycle instructors teaching in the same class, guaranteeing you'll connect with at least one of them. All instructors communicate and teach differently. You need to find the one who speaks your "teaching language."

The other benefit with that number of instructors is you stand a good chance of getting some proper attention. A ratio of one instructor to five riders is ideal. The other thing to know about instructors is they may have a specialty. A racer with lots of trophies, a dirt bike rider whose motorcycle has loads of mud under the guards, or a retired motorcycle cop can make an excellent instructor, but keep in mind that riding and teaching are two different skill sets. Try to align yourself with an instructor, or ideally multiple instructors, who do the type of riding you want to do.

Whether you end up riding your motorcycle on-road or off, one thing you'll definitely want to inquire about at this stage is what bikes the school uses and what protective clothing is offered. Be sure to seek a program that uses newer model motorcycles that are regularly inspected and certified according to local safety laws and one that provides a helmet, gloves, and jacket. Expect these to be suitably scuffed, but know they'll take care of your immediate safety, while also providing an excellent opportunity for you to try out bikes and equipment that you might want to go on to purchase. On the topic of clothing, be prepared to show up wearing jeans and shoes or boots that cover your ankle. If you show up in slip-on shoes and sweatpants, expect to be sent home.

Like most things, a good training program is as much about what you're prepared to put into your learning, as the value of the course itself. The good news is there are plenty of things you can do to make sure you're the star of the class. One simple thing is to ride a bicycle. If I could get every student to ride a bicycle for an hour or two before their motorcycle safety course, I'm certain I'd have a 99 percent pass rate. Think about it: a bicycle, like a motorcycle, has two wheels, and if you can't operate a ten-pound bicycle, then how are you going to operate a 300 to 800-pound motorcycle?

It sounds obvious, but be sure to get a good night's sleep the night before, put your phone down, wear the right clothing (layering up to keep warm and bringing a change of clothes in case it rains), drink lots of water, and don't eat heavy meals during the course. Bottom line: you're there to learn, so don't engage in anything that's going to sap your energy and distract you from taking the training.

Finally, don't take things personally. The instructors will be yelling because the helmets and motorcycles make it harder to hear. Don't think for a moment they hate you; they just want you to be safe. As for the other students, be friendly with them. These are your first riding buddies. Think about starting a group on Facebook or WhatsApp. New riders never have enough people to ride with.

If you're still hungry for more at the end of a basic training program, there are always further courses you can take. One option is to undertake a practice road test under the watchful eye of an instructor. This fine-tunes your skills ahead of the real deal. Alternatively, you can sign yourself up for an instructor-led road ride. Around three hours long, the ride will provide you with guidance and feedback from an instructor as you weave your way through your city's roads. Lastly, there's always advanced motorcycle training courses. These teach and hone more complicated motorcycle skills, such as cornering and braking at different speeds. The sooner you start taking any of these riding courses, the quicker you'll become a much safer rider.

My first advanced rider training was three years after I learned to ride. It was a course designed to teach me how to become a motorcycle racer (I'd won it at a motorcycle charity event). As I spent all my time riding with riders more skilled than I, I thought I was a good rider, and so I was excited to take the course. As soon as my bike hit the track, however, I realized just how little I knew. Cornering, body positioning, and safe lines around a corner escaped me. While I had clocked many miles riding with others, I'd also picked up many bad habits; I had a lot of work to do. It took pairing me with a top racing instructor to wipe my riding slate clean. From that day on, I made advanced rider training a part of every riding season.

Basic or advanced training, it really doesn't matter: both will make you a safer rider and show you just how much you and your bike can do. Invest in your motorcycling future by taking the advanced training.

CHAPTER 3

GETTING
YOUR GEAR

I look tall, strong, and deceptively buff in my cobalt blue, white and black leather motorcycle gear. I even look like a super hero, a Power Ranger, in fact. Wherever I go, I command attention while wearing it. Even if that attention is just an enthusiastic wave from a little kid, I still can't help but feel special. What admirers don't know, however, is that my gear has nothing to do with vanity—well, not wholly—but, instead, with the fear of motorcycle riding I had at the outset. I was so scared about what I was getting myself into that I was dressing for the worst possible scenario. Knowing the gear offered protection gave me the confidence I needed to ride a high-powered engine on two wheels. "Dress for the slide, not the ride" is still my mantra, and I encourage you to adopt it, too.

DO RIDERS HAVE TO WEAR GEAR?

By law, there are only two things you need to ride a motorcycle: a helmet and your underwear. That law, however, is not a blanket one. You must wear underwear, but in two-thirds of the United States, you don't have to wear a helmet, and plenty of riders choose not to. As shocking as that is, there are plenty of reasons for it.

First, motorcycle gear is costly. When new riders aren't sure they're even going to enjoy riding, they're reluctant to spend the money it takes to get the full protective kit. Something to keep in mind when spending money on motorcycle gear, though, is the option of re-selling it. It's common to get 50-60 percent of the gear's original value back, and certainly, the cost of not wearing gear is far greater than the price of buying it. Another option is to buy used motorcycle gear. Found in consignment stores or on Craigslist, this option is great, as there is a big possibility the gear has barely been worn. The only thing I would not recommend buying is a used helmet. Those should be bought brand new. You never know the true history of a used helmet.

Another big deterrent for wearing motorcycle gear is the weather. Hot weather, cold weather, humidity and more can make motorcycle gear uncomfortable. The good news is these irritants can be managed, as there is plenty of motorcycle gear that allows the free flow of air to keep you cool while still protecting you. Look for perforated gear (with tiny holes throughout the jacket or pants) or gear with zippered panels for airflow. Avoiding black-colored gear and choosing light colors instead will also help. Black absorbs heat, while lighter colors reflect it. In cold conditions, every motorcyclist loves their heated motorcycle gear. Heated gear feels like wrapping a warm blanket, fresh from the clothes dryer, around you. Even with these options, there will be times when you feel uncomfortable in your motorcycle gear. This is where perseverance comes in. You can handle it. You certainly don't want to handle the result of not wearing it.

Riders often overlook motorcycle gear because it's restrictive. While it can feel like your ability to operate the motorcycle in gear is hindered, you will get used to this. Indeed, a motorcycle can be operated at an advanced level while wearing the tightest, most protective motorcycle gear. Besides, it's tight for a good reason. If you can move the padding and armor around too much, it will not protect you in the way it was designed.

There's also a cultural consideration at play in riders' relationships to motorcycle gear in that more often than not, motorcyclists are portrayed like Peter Fonda and Dennis Hopper in Easy Rider: freewheeling and helmet-less. You even see this among today's motorcycling YouTube stars. It's an image that's carefully choreographed. Most of today's riders mount cameras to their helmet so you see the highway or racetrack whizzing by but not necessarily any protective gear they might be wearing.

Don't be seduced by this kind of myth making. Wear protective gear. Our bodies have evolved to travel no faster than about twenty-five miles/forty kilometers per hour. Even at that speed, hitting something hard can hurt or kill you and, if you're going any faster, your bones and organs simply can't handle the force of the impact without some kind of protection. Nor can your skin. You'd never run as fast you could along the road and shoulder roll into the pavement. So, why would you hop on a motorcycle and risk the same thing at a higher speed?

WHAT GEAR SHOULD BE WORN?

I once rode without a helmet. Just once. I was riding with friends in the state of Wyoming in the incredible Yellowstone National Park. There were many places to stop and visit, and so we decided to skip the helmets between stops. I get the appeal of the wind in your face, but it was then I discovered that the wind can also be full of debris. If you look at the front of your car, you'll see lots of little chips from bugs and rocks that hit the bumper and windscreen as you drive at high speed. Imagine what those same bugs and rocks do to your face when they hit you. Then imagine what an oncoming car would do. My experience of riding without a helmet was a short one, but it was long enough to not understand the appeal of riding helmet less. Enough said. The first piece of gear you should buy is a helmet.

Helmets are designed to protect your head from extreme G forces and objects it might be subject to. The helmet's fit and the safety standard it meets is your priority. Your helmet should fit you tightly but still be comfortable enough to wear all day. It takes time to find the right helmet to fit your head. A helmet fitting can take up to an hour. Don't be tempted to rush it.

There are three internationally recognized standards for helmets to keep an eye out for. Minimally, for a helmet to be legal in the United States and Canada, it should carry a Department of Transportation (DOT) sticker. Additional standards include Snell and ECE 22.05 (a standard created by the Economic Commission for Europe), which are higher, so consider getting a DOT helmet with one of these. A helmet is only safe for one impact. If your head hits the ground in a motorcycle crash, consider that helmet done. If you drop your helmet off your motorcycle or a table, however, it will probably be fine. There is no way to be certain about this, though, so just be careful where you place your helmet. I've never had a problem putting my helmet on the ground. It's not that dirty, and besides, the ground is probably the safest place for it.

The style of helmet is also a consideration and here you have several options based on what motorcycle you ride. Traditionally, sport bikers tend to wear full-face helmets. Touring motorcyclists wear modular, and the cruiser crowd can be seen in beanies, half-helmets and three-quarter helmets. Fashion might influence what you wear, but remember: crashes and accidents do not care. Feeling the wind on your face is a high risk considering almost 50 percent of scrapes and impacts happen in the facial area. Regardless of what motorcycle you ride, full-face helmets are the way to go. With the vast variety of designs and styles, you can find a full-face helmet that will match the look of your motorcycle. If you do deem it worth the risk to wear a helmet with no facial protection, try eating your dinner through a straw. If you crash, that might be a reality.

Your next purchase should be a motorcycle jacket—a recognized motorcycle jacket—and not any old jacket you found in your closet. This jacket will protect you from everything from scrapes to sunburn, so choose one that's made from a very dense fabric that's designed for motorcycling. Leather jackets, stitched from the hides of kangaroo to cow, offer the best protection and can be crashed in multiple times. They can be warm to wear, however, so be sure to look for ones with zippers or air flow vents. Textile is a close second to leather, and it's cheaper. Like the seat belt in your car, textile jackets have all the safety features you could need, plus extra layers to keep warm and dry. They also come with lots of pockets. Don't be tempted to put too much in them. If you were to crash, you wouldn't want to fall on pockets full of things. If you think riding around in a T-shirt and shorts is a good idea, mesh gear is your hot weather option. Mesh jackets are made of dense fabric and contain armor but not so much that airflow is compromised. These jackets won't perform well for safety versus leather and textile, but they will be far better than no gear at all.

The key thing with jackets is their fit. When trying on a motorcycle jacket, you want a tighter fit. If the jacket is too roomy, the padding and armor might move off the areas it is trying to protect. Still, try to leave a little room for a heated jacket or sweater for colder riding. You also have the option of buying tougher padding and armor to upgrade your motorcycle jacket. Higher-level back protection (CE2) can replace the back armor your jacket came with, or, you can buy something separate that you wear under your jacket. You'll find a big difference in the back armor a jacket comes with versus what you can buy. On a final note, notice how the arms of the jacket naturally curve with your arms. This ensures your joints remain in the right places if you take a tumble. Motorcycle jackets are excellent at protecting you against soft tissue injuries, keeping your arms and shoulders where they should be.

Motorcycle gloves should follow on your list of purchases. For me, the sleeves of a motorcycle jacket bought off the rack are always two to three inches too short. I've always bought gauntlet gloves, the longest gloves you can buy, to cover my wrists. I didn't realize it at the time, but these are the best you can buy. Think about it: if you've ever fallen and scraped the palms of your hands, you know how much that hurts. Do that when riding your motorcycle at any speed, and you will be grateful for having that little extra protection from your long gloves. As with other gear, leather is your best bet for material. You will also want extra knuckle protection, a nice snug fit, and a Velcro fastener to ensure your gloves stay on well. You may find wearing gloves makes using the motorcycle controls restrictive. Tough! This is something you need to get used to. If professional riders can ride their motorcycles at high rates of speed with the biggest and thickest gloves, you can manage riding at street speeds in a street glove.

Your legs make up a big part of your body, so let's not forget motorcycle pants. They are a must-have. Leaving all jokes of leather pants aside, they're worth it. Like your jacket, your pants need to be tight but comfortable. The knee and hip armor should stay in place, so if you can move them around, try a different size and style. Know that the style of motorcycle pants is purposeful. Not only does the style make the pants more comfortable when you sit on your motorcycle, it ensures your knees stay in the right direction. Don't think for a second your regular pair of jeans is tough enough to substitute for motorcycle pants. They're not. Today's jeans are made of thin, ultra light material and will not cut it. There is the option of motorcycle jeans. These jeans are thicker and made of tough materials like Kevlar. Speaking of materials, motorcycle pants also come in materials like mesh, textile, and leather. If you go the leather route, make sure you get pants with good airflow, as they can get quite warm on a hot day.

While motorcycle boots have segued into mainstream fashion, there's an altogether good reason to wear them while riding: your feet will hit the ground first—or a close second to your hands and hips—if you take a tumble. A full-size motorcycle boot will cover your foot and your ankle and even go part way up your calf muscle to cover and protect almost 25 percent of the bones in your body along with your tendons and ligaments. Motorcycle boots come in all shapes and sizes. They fasten with zippers, Velcro, straps, and even laces. Laces can come loose so ensure you tie a knot good enough to never come undone. Like gloves, I recommend getting boots with the most amount of coverage, as your ankle is a delicate area. You'll notice a full-sized motorcycle boot is quite stiff. It's not quite as stiff as a ski boot but as stiff as a snowboard boot. This stiffness protects your foot from being thrashed and twisted in a fall.

If not subject to an almighty crash, your helmet, leather jacket, gloves, pants, and boots should last up to five years if you look after them properly. Store your gear in a dry place out of the sun and not in a heap on the floor. Give your gear a cleaning now and again by putting it in the washing machine. Front loading washers work best, as they're much gentler and won't twist or stretch your gear like a top loader. Be sure to take out the armor, turn the clothing inside out and set the washer to a delicate wash setting. Then, hang the items to dry and apply leather conditioner if your gear is leather.

If you're going to venture off the main street and onto a track or dirt road, you'll need different gear. Typically, sport biking gear is characterized by bright colors and extreme designs. That said, make sure that whatever it looks like, you're in a full-faced helmet shaped for speed, head-to-toe leather, and full-sized boots.

Dirt biking, meanwhile, is going to see you in looser-fitting protective gear, ideally made from a lighter textile to ensure you have a greater range of motion. Given that you use your foot more often on a dirt bike, you're also going to need a different style of boot. Boots should come to calf height and be of heavier-duty material to protect your feet from rocks and gravel.

The cruiser crowd prefers black leather jackets and vests. It's worth mentioning that while black looks cool, it's the least visible color to wear. What's more, it absorbs the most amount of heat from the sun. My gear is a blend of white, grey, and blue with some blacks. This is key in keeping cool in the hot sun. The perforated holes also allow for more air-flow, which is great for hot weather. Just because you ride in a hot climate doesn't exclude you from wearing gear. A motorcycle crash is no different on a hot day versus a cold one. Resist the urge to wear a T-shirt, sandals, and flip-flops.

HOW TO GET THE BEST DEAL

So, you have your shopping list. Time to go shopping. It's likely you'll end up at one of the bigger motorcycle gear stores. There you will be confronted by dozens of different brands, all carrying different price tags. Guaranteed this will throw you into a quandary. Should you buy the most expensive stuff from the big brands, or does the cheaper stuff offer just as good protection? The short answer is:

maybe. Maybe's not great when you consider the odds of a new rider making a mistake; the odds are higher. This being so, I highly recommend spending more money than you're comfortable with and getting the best protection you can. For just a helmet, jacket, and gloves, you'll end up paying around $300 and up. For head to toe coverage, you're looking at upwards of $800.

Choosing gear from reputable stores and brands such as Alpinestars, Dainese, Joe Rocket, REV'IT or Scorpion is a wise way to go, but it will make a dent in that $800 quickly. One way around this is to ask for a package deal. Think about it. As a new rider with gear needs now and into the future, you're a potential asset for any store. And besides, the worst they'll say to you is no. Know that the more gear you buy with them, the more of a deal they should offer. Be sure to check out a few stores to see who'll give you the best deal on what you need. It's tough for a store to stock the entire inventory that fits your size, so be prepared to be patient and place an order to get the right size for you.

Buying your gear online can lead to some great deals, but obviously, it's tough to gauge if the gear is going to fit. Thankfully, online shopping has excellent return policies so you can buy it, try it on and send it back if necessary. Do not buy a helmet online unless you know for sure that the brand and size fits your head. I know a Scorpion XL helmet fits my head perfectly, so I will buy a season ending deal on that helmet every few years.

You'll soon find you're collecting all sorts of motorcycle gear, as you'll want to have the right stuff to be comfortable, cool, and safe. If you ever find your closet getting too full, you can always resell it. There is a good market for people wanting to buy used gear. You can also pay it forward and help a new rider out with hand-me-down gear. Wherever you end up buying your gear and however much you spend on it, don't underestimate the value it will bring you in confidence alone. Dressing for motorcycling is no different from dressing to go to a party or a work function. If you're wearing clothes that are appropriate and that fit and look good, you'll feel a lot better about the whole experience.

REMEMBER: YOU'RE NO IRONMAN

Motorcycle gear is amazing. You'd think it has super hero qualities given the damage it protects us against, but make no mistake: we are not Ironman when we wear it. We are still phenomenally vulnerable. I realized this in 2007. I was part of a group of twelve riders touring the Cascade Mountains in Washington. It's an incredible road, and it was made more incredible by having the road almost to ourselves. We were quite spread out and didn't immediately realize that one rider was missing. When we went back to find our buddy, he had gone off the road. Not just off the road but down the mountainside. His motorcycle had hit every rock and boulder on the way down and there was not a part of his motorcycle or gear that had not borne the brunt of this. It was a terrible scene, but he was alive. It took a long time for help to arrive and even longer to get him up and out of there. It transpired that he broke his leg, pelvis, and back (thankfully, he didn't sustain paralysis). Clearly, his gear had done everything it could to protect him, and it had done it very well. While he didn't have a head or joint injury, he did have a lengthy recovery. The following season he was healthy enough to ride again. And he did.

Some people have to take a fall wearing no motorcycle gear in order to realize how important it is to wear it. Avoid that costly mistake and don't let a moment in which you skip the motorcycle gear, bring about a lifetime of regret.

CHAPTER 4

FINDING YOUR FIRST MOTORCYCLE

When I bought my first motorcycle, I was fortunate. Already enrolled in a motorcycle safety course, one of my fellow students who worked at a dealer offered to sell me a used 1989 Honda CB1 off her lot. I went to look at it. It was a smaller bike at 400ccs, but I knew it was just the right size for my first motorcycle. So, despite it being the only bike I'd looked at, I bought it on the spot. Since it was my first motorcycle, I figured almost any bike would do. And I was right. It might have been small, but it was still scary and thrilling to ride. I was riding and that's all that mattered to me. As first motorcycle stories go, my bike baptism was a harmless one.

Such was not the case for John, a former student of mine. John, in his ignorance, bought a 600cc sport bike right after completing his motorcycle safety course. The 600cc super sports (or larger) are more at home on a racetrack than a suburban freeway. One day while sitting on his new bike in traffic, he hit a bump. The bump was enough to blip the throttle and shoot the bike forward unexpectedly. Terrified, he slammed on his brakes causing the front tire to lock, slide out, and careen into the car in front. Fortunately for John, he left the scene unscathed. Unfortunately for John's beast of a bike, it broke into three hundred pieces in front of him. We call these types of accidents Tupperware parties: plastic bits everywhere.

Being into motorcycles as much in the beginning as I still am now, I understand how excited a new rider is to purchase their first bike. But it's the little mistakes, made early, that can turn into big mistakes later, as John found out. A little knowledge and forethought is key, if you don't wish to break the bank, yourself, or your new motorcycle, and that's what this chapter is intended to give you.

WHEN AND HOW SHOULD NEW RIDERS START LOOKING FOR THEIR FIRST BIKE?

It's no coincidence that John and I bought our first bike after undertaking a motorcycle safety course. This is usually the point in a beginning rider's journey when they are sufficiently confident with riding and have had enough exposure to a range of bikes to make what is a significant purchase. Yes, the purchase is significant financially, but it's more significant in terms of a new rider's learning curve. Once you've learned all the basic and necessary skills in a motorcycle safety course, you need to get on the road and start practicing those skills immediately. If you don't buy a motorcycle directly after the course, it will take longer to genuinely learn how to ride a bike. If you don't use those new skills, you'll lose them.

When looking for your first bike, start by riding as many bikes as possible during your motorcycle safety course. You can dream about a bike as much as you like, but until you actually ride it, you really don't know if it's comfortable, manageable, and a good fit for you.

Before you get too caught up in this research, establish a budget. Between $3,000 and $5,000 is typically what new riders spend on a first bike. Working out what you're prepared to spend is important, as it will dictate what you can ultimately go on to buy: a big or small bike, a road or sports bike, or a new or used bike. When deciding on a figure, remember that your first motorcycle is a learning bike and there's a strong possibility you'll outgrow it within three months to six months. What's more, given you're still relatively new to riding, you're going to scratch and drop your bike, making buying the biggest, newest, shiniest, most amazing motorcycle on the market not the smartest purchase.

Be aware that when you do make it to the dealer's lot, your budget will be tested. It's a dealer's job to get you what you want, not necessarily what you need. Typically, they'll stretch your budget by offering you a motorcycle loan and before you know it, you're leaving the dealership with a wildly different and more expensive motorcycle than you thought you would buy.

Whatever you decide to spend on your bike, consider buying a smaller one first. If you're after a sports bike, consider something with an engine less than 600cc. If you want a cruiser, 800cc or less is a good starting point. With dirt bikes, think about 450cc or less. Different styles of bikes perform differently depending on the engine they're equipped with. Sports bikes can generate a lot of power with smaller engines. Cruisers and dirt bikes generate their power early so they can't go as fast as sports bikes. Whatever you choose, remember that a small bike is lighter and more manageable, enabling you to feel comfortable and gain confidence quicker. A big, heavier motorcycle comes with a steep learning curve and poses a big threat not only to your budget but to your safety as a new rider.

Buying a small bike, incidentally, is also a smart move when it comes to re-selling it, as the biggest market for bikes is a new rider looking for a small motorcycle. Providing you're not a complete disaster of a rider, and it's not a scrap heap of parts, someone will be willing to buy your small bike for more or less what you bought it for.

The decision to purchase a road or sports bike comes down to how you intend to use your bike. Be clear about this before making any purchase and choose the right tool for the job. As exciting as a sports bike may look, they normally pack more power and don't feel comfortable to ride at lower speeds on city streets.

Discomfort isn't unique to a sports bike; you can experience it on a road bike, too. Before you throw your wallet at any motorcycle, you should sit on it and test it for fit and comfort. You'll be most comfortable on a motorcycle if your feet can touch the ground. If you can only touch the ground with the tip of your toes or balls of your feet, it's still possible to ride a motorcycle; it will just require better balance and more control. Be sure to wear your motorcycle boots when testing the bike for fit, as they have a higher sole than regular shoes. Notice also while you're sitting on the bike how your back feels. If it hurts after the first two minutes, riding for long periods will be tough. Finally, consider how your arms rest in relation to the handlebars. Your arms should be in a relaxed position, not straight out. If you have really short arms and have to strain to reach for the controls, you won't have the full range of motion you need to be able to operate the bike safely. The best height to fit all motorcycles seems to be five-feet-nine inches (175 centimeters).

Speaking of short arms, one of the most common questions I get asked is, "Am I too short to ride?" The quick answer is: absolutely not. There are lots of little tricks you can do to make motorcycling easier if you are around five feet (150 centimeters) tall. You'll want to start with a smaller motor-cycle, something like a Honda Grom or a small 250cc cruiser. These have very low seat heights and are light. Since you are shorter, balance is going to be more challenging. You'll want the easiest motorcycle to start with to get a good foundation in balance. Once you graduate to a larger motorcycle, you can get a custom seat that is thinner, which will drop the seat height. A lowering link, which lowers the clearance, will also help. Some people don't recommend this, but unless you're planning to go racing, it shouldn't be a problem. Finally, think about purchasing boots with a thicker sole to add the extra inches in height.

What about tall riders? If you are six feet (180 centimeters) or taller, the number of motorcycles you will feel comfortable on are limited. That said, bigger cruisers, adventure bikes, sport-touring bikes, and upright sports bikes, would offer you the greatest comfort. I ride a Kawasaki ZX10R and by customizing it with a set of more upright handlebars, this bike offers a more pleasant ride for my six feet two inch (189 centimeters) frame.

If you are curious what motorcycle might best fit your frame, go to: http://cycle-ergo.com/. This is an excellent website that simulates your posture on every style of motorcycle by simply entering your height into their calculator. It's great in the reconnaissance stage of motorcycle shopping, but don't be tempted to let it replace sitting on a bike and riding it.

WHAT NEW RIDERS SHOULD LOOK FOR IN A NEW MOTORCYCLE

When I started motorcycle riding in 2005, I knew I wanted to buy a small bike. It just made sense to start small and work my way up. At the time, bikes with a 600cc and larger engine were the most readily available. I knew I could probably handle a motorcycle of that size, but I wanted to be as safe as I could, so I went back in time to find my 400cc 1989 Honda CB1. When this bike was brand new, I was nine years old. That didn't bother me, though—it was perfect being $2,900 and within my budget. Nowadays, I could buy a brand new 300cc motorcycle for around $4,000, as every manufacturer has a line of smaller cc motorcycles. With all the choice of new, affordable bikes with the latest technology and safety features, there's never been a better time to get into motorcycles. Indeed, a new rider has never had so many options for bikes costing $5,000 or less. So where does one begin to even pick a new motorcycle?

Other than size, brand is key. Harley Davidson is one of the biggest and most recognized brands out there. No brand has been better at selling the lifestyle of motorcycling than Harley. Harley specializes in cruisers and touring cruisers with larger engines. They do have smaller motorcycles to start out with, though. The Harley Street 500 and 750, 883 Iron, Street Rod, and SuperLow would be good first bikes. While small, they will still feel like a lot of motorcycle as their engines still pack a lot of power. The average cost of a Harley Davidson is more than other brands on the market as you're paying for the Harley name. Unfortunately, the brand tends to be the last to embrace rider technology such as ABS, traction control, and suspension adjustments. Do know they are not the most reliable of bikes and will require more maintenance visits than the average motorcycle. Don't let that dissuade you from a Harley, though. Their dealer network is the largest and most extensive, and they really support their riders.

Honda is a very familiar brand for both cars and motorcycles. They hail from Japan and build nothing but quality, reliable motorcycles. With a wide variety of bikes to choose from, everything from dirt bikes to sport bikes and cruisers to touring, Honda has something for every rider. Their motors

are so efficient that some riders think they're not as excit-
ing as other motorcycles. I think you can't go wrong with a
Honda motorcycle. Their new rider options are the CBR300,
CBR500, CB300F, CB500F, Grom, CB500X, Rebel 300/500,
CRF230, and a few other smaller options. As early adopt-
ers of new technology and safety features, you'll often see
Hondas used in most motorcycle safety schools.

Kawasaki is another Japanese brand with great reliability
and quality. Like Honda, they have the same wide variety of
choices across all styles of motorcycles. Their fit and finish
may not be quite up to Honda and Yamaha's standards,
but that might be more my personal preference. I do find
Kawasaki has the best value for your motorcycling dollars,
and quite often, they have great dealer incentives to make it
even more cost-effective. My last two motorcycles have been
Kawasakis because they offered affordability and a ton of
features. They have plenty of new rider options including the
Ninja 300, Versys 300, Z125 Pro, Vulvcan S, and ERN-6. You'll
find all the latest technology on Kawasaki motorcycles, too.

Yamaha is the more extreme Japanese brand with edgy
designs and interesting engine configurations. They still have
excellent reliability and their fit and finish is nicer than the
Kawasaki. Yamaha has models across all styles of riding, but
their pricing can be higher than their competitors. You'll have
plenty of new rider options with the R3, XT250, TW200, and

Vstar 250. Once you're ready to move up to the larger motor-cycle, the FZ10 and the FZ09 are quite interesting models in both design and engines. Yamaha also makes use of the newest technology, so you'll always be well taken care of.

Suzuki is the last of the Japanese brands, and they have lots of great options for first-time riders as well. These bikes don't quite have the reliability, technology, fit, and finish of the other Japanese brands but their pricing is very competitive. New rider models such as the SV650, TU250X, GW250, GSX250R, DRZ, Boulevard S40, and Vstrom 650 ensure you have lots to choose from as your first motorcycle.

If you're into European cars, you'll be happy to know BMW makes a wide variety of motorcycles, too. BMW leads the way in getting safety features into their motorcycles and was the first company to make ABS standard across all motorcycles. There are limited options for new riders: just the recently released BMW 310R and 310GS. BMW's larger motorcycle lineup, though, is quite large, so you'll have plenty to choose from when you buy your second or third motorcycle. Keep in mind: pricing and maintenance is higher on BMWs, but the bikes will be fitted with the latest technology and safety features. Just like their cars, BMW motorcycles make for one amazing ride.

Ducati are the Ferrari of the motorcycle world. Some of

the most exciting motorcycles come from this Italian brand, as their race technology tends to end up on their street models. Since these are advanced motorcycles, they do require advanced riding skills. Do not go right to a Panigale or a Diavel as your first motorcycle. In fact, most of their models are not new-rider friendly with the exception of the Scrambler Sixty2. If you absolutely must have a Ducati as your first motorcycle, start with the Sixty2 and then trade it up. Consider the Sixty2 an entry into the velvet roped, red carpet of the hottest night club, for along with all this excitement comes a higher price tag and high maintenance costs. That said, you'll never regret buying a Ducati. Ducati makes motorcycles that move your soul, not just your body.

Aprilia is another Italian brand. If Ducati is the Ferrari of the motorcycle world, an Aprilia might be considered the Lamborghini. They do not build new-rider friendly motorcycles, so these are not your best choice for a first motorcycle. They are exciting to ride, though, as Aprilia really embraces the V4 engine configuration on their race replica machines. Just like Ducati, the prices and maintenance will be higher.

KTM is another European brand based out of Austria. Just like Ducati, they have some very exciting models. They're known for dirt and motocross motorcycles and have the championship trophies to show for it. They do have plenty of street models, too, though, that offer the latest technology, creative design and powerful engines. New rider models are the RC390 and the Duke 390. Like Ducati and Aprilia, their pricing is higher with more maintenance required to keep them running.

Triumph is the British motorcycle of choice. They don't quite cater to new riders, as all their motorcycles are on the larger side, but the T100 might be possible if you take to riding quickly. Triumph uses the triple cylinder engine on most of their motorcycles producing a bike with a unique raw sound and lots of power. While British vehicles do not have a good history with reliability, the Triumphs are a solid brand. You will get decent reliability and maintenance requirements with these bikes. Technology comes a little later with Triumph, but they do value the simple nature of motorcycling.

WHAT NEW RIDERS SHOULD LOOK FOR IN A USED MOTORCYCLE

Budget will likely be the overriding factor in seeking out a used motorcycle. A used bike is a great economical option for a new rider, but it does require you to have your eyes wide open while you look for the perfect one. And I mean open.

Again, you'll want to narrow the search down by brand initially. American, Japanese, Italian, German, Austrian or British motorcycle, though, it doesn't matter. When you're in front of the bike, look closely at the condition it's in. If it has some surface scrapes or bumps, that's completely fine; it's the hidden ones that might suggest the bike has been in an accident that are more concerning. Run your fingers along the edge of the handlebars and mirrors or down low by the controls; if you feel scrapes or scuffs, there's a good chance the bike has hit the ground. If the seller does not disclose this, you might wisely wonder what else the seller is hiding and walk away.

How clean the bike is, is another good indication of the general condition of the motorcycle. A lot of motorcycles have a chain by the rear wheel, which generates the speed to propel the bike forward. If the rear chain is clean and well lubricated, then you're looking at a bike well taken care of. If the chain is very dirty, dry or even rusty, it could suggest neglect and potentially a faulty bike.

Examining the tires can also help determine the condition of a bike. Start by scanning the tires for nails or other objects and look at how the tread has held up. More importantly, calculate how old the tires are. All motorcycle tires have a manufacturing date on them; a four-digit code with the first two digits representing the week of the year and the last two representing the year. If it says 2415, for example, it was made in the 24th week of 2015. If a tire is older than five years, you shouldn't be riding on it and it will need to be replaced. As a motorcycle tire ages, the compound it's made from hardens, and the harder it becomes, the less traction it will give you. A brand-new motorcycle tire, in contrast, will feel very soft, and it's this that provides traction on the road.

Next, you'll want to sit on the bike, turn the key and check if the signals and the head and taillights are working. You might also take a look at the oil. The oil is on the right side of the bike. If the oil looks clean, then the owner has likely changed it and probably taken care of the bike more broadly. If the oil is very dark, it's not necessarily a bad thing, if everything else is in top shape. It just means you'll have to change the oil sooner rather than later.

Finally, note the motorcycle's mileage. If it's less than 5,000 kilometers/3,000 miles, you're probably looking at a bike with a lot of life still left in it. That said, a bike that's over five years old with very low mileage has likely spent most of its time sitting and may not be a good purchase. On the opposite end of the continuum, a motorcycle that's clocked up over 20,000 kilometers/12,500 miles (or higher) might be just fine if it's been well maintained. The smartest move is to ask for maintenance records.

Time and usage affects every motorcycle, and there's a lot to look for to determine the health of a used motorcycle. If you're nervous at all, hire a mechanic or someone who knows more about motorcycles than you do to go bike shopping with you. Even if they cost $100, that $100 can very well save you hundreds or even thousands of dollars on future repair bills. One final piece of insurance would be to inquire if the dealer (presuming you're going this route and not buying from a private seller) offers a warranty. Typically, these run from thirty to ninety days.

MORE RIDING, LESS REPAIRS

Over the years, I've had plenty of excited students show me their new ride. As an instructor, this never gets old. The happiest riders always seem to be the ones with the new or nearly new motorcycles. Bikes under three years old have low mileage and are reliable and relatively affordable. Older bikes might seem like a good deal, unfortunately, they rarely are. One of my students fell for an older bike, which appeared to work great when she bought it. It soon broke down, however, and she wound up spending more time repairing her motorcycle than riding it. This is incredibly frustrating for a new rider, who just wants to ride. Unless you love hunting down motorcycle parts or have ambitions of learning to be a motorcycle mechanic, spend the extra money on a newer bike.

Remember, as a beginner rider you need to get out there and ride to sharpen your newly acquired skills. Naturally, you'll want to make the best possible decision when buying something as expensive as a motorcycle, but don't worry about making the perfect one. Stick to your budget and don't buy anything too big or old, but other than that, just buy a bike that's reliable, easy to ride, and makes you feel excited. Your next bike, or even your third bike should be your dream bike. Between now and then, you have lots of learning and discovering to do.

FINANCING YOUR FIRST MOTORCYCLE

The day you get a new, or new to you, motorcycle is the best of days. I distinctly remember the days I've bought a new motorcycle for one big reason: along with that motorcycle came a price tag. I didn't always have the money to pay that price tag, but I was always smart about it, unlike one of my students.

The Kawasaki Ninja 300 is a common new rider sports bike. Affordable and fun, brand new, the bike is around $5,000. Seduced by the Ninja's design and reputation, my student bought a special edition version of it for over $7,000 (out the door, taxes and fees in). It was an amount he'd secured an eight-year loan for. His loan payment was a tiny $120 a month so on the face of it, he thought he'd scored a great deal. What he didn't realize was $90 of that repayment was interest, but worse, he would be paying for the bike long after he was likely to have fallen out of love with it, and traded it in for another.

How to finance your first motorcycle can be as dicey as crashing your motorcycle. They both happen fast, but the consequences can be long-lasting. This chapter will survey your options for financing a motorcycle and hopefully, save you some money and heartache.

HOW A NEW RIDER SHOULD BUY THEIR FIRST MOTORCYCLE

Prior to opening 1st Gear Motorcycle School, I was a financial planner for twelve years. In that time, I learned a thing or two about money. I dealt mostly with the finances of families, and, by far, the biggest challenges to their monthly budget were the loans, lines of credit, and ridiculous mortgages that some had entered into. It's easy to get into debt for the necessities of life, but almost easier for the luxuries, like motorcycles, for we want them and we want them now.

To avoid falling into the same trap as my student and some of my former clients, the smartest way to finance your first motorcycle is to pay cash and buy it outright. While easier said than done, paying interest on a loan for something that's pure fun isn't smart, particularly when you think of necessary loans you may have to take out for things like houses or cars.

If paying by cash is not an option, you have three alternatives. The first is to take out a loan from the motorcycle dealer. As with all loans, it's good general advice to seek as little interest and as short a repayment term as possible—no longer than a three-year term. You'll achieve this by putting down as large a deposit as you can, ideally 25 percent of the motorcycle. Your down payment and subsequent monthly payments should always hurt a little; this way, you're incentivized to clear the debt as quickly as possible.

A word of warning: if your finances are not as solid as they could be, you need a restrictive, painful loan plan to keep yourself honest. A motorcycle dealer isn't going to help you with your money worries given their goal is to get you purchasing a motorcycle as quickly as possible. There's a secondary reason you'll want to get in and out of your loan quickly: motorcycles devalue fast. If you get a 100 percent loan, your motorcycle will devalue quicker than the time it takes you to pay off the loan. In other words, what you owe will be dishearteningly greater than the value of your bike.

I've included tables to illustrate what a terrible, better, and best loan looks like. Study these tables, and you'll see how much interest you could be paying, per payment, over the life of the loan. Take them to the dealer and display some confidence when asking: what is the interest rate? And what are the terms?

If the motorcycle dealer doesn't offer financing, your next option is to ask your bank for a line of credit. A line of credit is a low interest bank account that allows you to go into the negative, providing you don't exceed the maximum amount set in the agreement and you meet the bank's other require-ments. Be cautious! A line of credit can be easy money if used undisciplined. There is no time limit to pay off the balance, and you can easily borrow more money with a few keystrokes of your computer or smartphone.

I used a line of credit, as well as some savings, for both my first and second motorcycles. My first bike cost $3,000 and my second, $5,000; both relatively small amounts that I was able to pay back within a year. Aside from ease of repayment, the other good thing about small, inexpensive motorcycles are they don't have a lot of room to go down in value. When you get into larger, more costly bikes, the number of people who will want to buy your used bike shrinks, ensuring their depreciation in value.

If your bank won't offer you a line of credit, option three is to ask for a loan. It is much easier to get a loan from a bank when you put money down (ideally 25 percent) and you're not asking the bank to finance one-hundred percent of the purchase. If they do fund one-hundred percent of your motorcycle, then know that your interest rate will be higher. As with asking your motorcycle dealer for a loan, the same rules apply. Go equipped with your terrible, better, and best loan tables and be prepared to ask some tough questions about interest rates and terms.

TERRIBLE LOANS

Eight-year loan for $12,650 with $0 down payment at 7.79 percent interest

	MONTHLY PAYMENT	INTEREST	CAPITAL	ENDING BALANCE
1	$177.48	$82.12	$95.36	$12,554.64
2	$177.48	$81.50	$95.98	$12,458.66
3	$177.48	$80.88	$96.60	$12,362.05
4	$177.48	$80.25	$97.23	$12,264.82
5	$177.48	$79.62	$97.86	$12,166.96
6	$177.48	$78.98	$98.50	$12,068.46
7	$177.48	$78.34	$99.14	$11,969.32
8	$177.48	$77.70	$99.78	$11,869.54
9	$177.48	$77.05	$100.43	$11,769.11
10	$177.48	$76.40	$101.08	$11,668.03
11	$177.48	$75.74	$101.74	$11,566.30
12	$177.48	$75.08	$102.40	$11,463.90
13	$177.48	$74.42	$103.06	$11,360.84
14	$177.48	$73.75	$103.73	$11,257.11
15	$177.48	$73.08	$104.40	$11,152.70
16	$177.48	$72.40	$105.08	$11,047.62
17	$177.48	$71.72	$105.76	$10,941.86
18	$177.48	$71.03	$106.45	$10,835.40
19	$177.48	$70.34	$107.14	$10,728.26
20	$177.48	$69.64	$107.84	$10,620.43
21	$177.48	$68.94	$108.54	$10,511.89
22	$177.48	$68.24	$109.24	$10,402.65
23	$177.48	$67.53	$109.95	$10,292.69
24	$177.48	$66.82	$110.66	$10,182.03
		$1,791.57		

- After two years, you have paid $1,791.57 in interest.
- You owe more money than the motorcycle is worth after two years.
- Note that more interest is paid in the first year.
- Note that the interest and principal paid is almost the same at the start.

Eight-year loan for $7,000 with $0 down payment at 7.79 percent interest

	MONTHLY PAYMENT	INTEREST	CAPITAL	ENDING BALANCE
1	$98.21	$45.44	$52.77	$6,947.23
2	$98.21	$45.10	$53.11	$6,894.12
3	$98.21	$44.75	$53.46	$6,840.66
4	$98.21	$44.41	$53.80	$6,786.86
5	$98.21	$44.06	$54.15	$6,732.70
6	$98.21	$43.71	$54.50	$6,678.20
7	$98.21	$43.35	$54.86	$6,623.34
8	$98.21	$43.00	$55.21	$6,568.13
9	$98.21	$42.64	$55.57	$6,512.55
10	$98.21	$42.28	$55.93	$6,456.62
11	$98.21	$41.91	$56.30	$6,400.32
12	$98.21	$41.55	$56.66	$6,343.66
13	$98.21	$41.18	$57.03	$6,286.63
14	$98.21	$40.81	$57.40	$6,229.23
15	$98.21	$40.44	$57.77	$6,171.46
16	$98.21	$40.06	$58.15	$6,113.31
17	$98.21	$39.69	$58.53	$6,054.78
18	$98.21	$39.31	$58.91	$5,995.88
19	$98.21	$38.92	$59.29	$5,936.59
20	$98.21	$38.54	$59.67	$5,876.92
21	$98.21	$38.15	$60.06	$5,816.85
22	$98.21	$37.76	$60.45	$5,756.40
23	$98.21	$37.37	$60.84	$5,695.56
24	$98.21	$36.97	$61.24	$5,634.32
		$991.40		

- After two years, you have paid $991.40 in interest.
- You owe more money than the motorcycle is worth after two years.
- Note that more interest is paid in the first year.
- Note that the interest and principal paid is almost the same at the start.

BETTER LOAN

Five-year loan for $12,650 with $1,000 down payment at 7.79 percent interest

	MONTHLY PAYMENT	INTEREST	CAPITAL	ENDING BALANCE
1	$235.05	$75.63	$159.42	$11,490.58
2	$235.05	$74.59	$160.46	$11,330.12
3	$235.05	$73.55	$161.50	$11,168.62
4	$235.05	$72.50	$162.55	$11,006.07
5	$235.05	$71.45	$163.60	$10,842.47
6	$235.05	$70.39	$164.67	$10,677.80
7	$235.05	$69.32	$165.73	$10,512.07
8	$235.05	$68.24	$166.81	$10,345.26
9	$235.05	$67.16	$167.89	$10,177.37
10	$235.05	$66.07	$168.98	$10,008.38
11	$235.05	$64.97	$170.08	$9,838.30
12	$235.05	$63.87	$171.18	$9,667.12
13	$235.05	$62.76	$172.30	$9,494.82
14	$235.05	$61.64	$173.41	$9,321.41
15	$235.05	$60.51	$174.54	$9,146.87
16	$235.05	$59.38	$175.67	$8,971.20
17	$235.05	$58.24	$176.81	$8,794.39
18	$235.05	$57.09	$177.96	$8,616.43
19	$235.05	$55.93	$179.12	$8,437.31
20	$235.05	$54.77	$180.28	$8,257.03
21	$235.05	$53.60	$181.45	$8,075.58
22	$235.05	$52.42	$182.63	$7,892.96
23	$235.05	$51.24	$183.81	$7,709.14
24	$235.05	$50.05	$185.01	$7,524.14
	$1,515.37			

- After two years, you have paid $1,515.37 in interest.
- You owe about what the motorcycle is worth after two years.
- Note that more interest is paid in the first year.
- Note that the interest is now half of what the principal payments are.

Five-year loan for $7,000 with $1,000 down payment at 7.79 percent interest

	MONTHLY PAYMENT	INTEREST	CAPITAL	ENDING BALANCE
1	$121.06	$38.95	$82.11	$5,917.89
2	$121.06	$38.42	$82.64	$5,835.25
3	$121.06	$37.88	$83.18	$5,752.08
4	$121.06	$37.34	$83.72	$5,668.36
5	$121.06	$36.80	$84.26	$5,584.10
6	$121.06	$36.25	$84.81	$5,499.30
7	$121.06	$35.70	$85.36	$5,413.94
8	$121.06	$35.15	$85.91	$5,328.03
9	$121.06	$34.59	$86.47	$5,241.56
10	$121.06	$34.03	$87.03	$5,154.53
11	$121.06	$33.46	$87.59	$5,066.94
12	$121.06	$32.89	$88.16	$4,978.77
13	$121.06	$32.32	$88.74	$4,890.04
14	$121.06	$31.74	$89.31	$4,800.73
15	$121.06	$31.16	$89.89	$4,710.84
16	$121.06	$30.58	$90.48	$4,620.36
17	$121.06	$29.99	$91.06	$4,529.30
18	$121.06	$29.40	$91.65	$4,437.64
19	$121.06	$28.81	$92.25	$4,345.40
20	$121.06	$28.21	$92.85	$4,252.55
21	$121.06	$27.61	$93.45	$4,159.10
22	$121.06	$27.00	$94.06	$4,065.04
23	$121.06	$26.39	$94.67	$3,970.37
24	$121.06	$25.77	$95.28	$3,875.09
		$780.44		

- After two years, you have paid $780.44 in interest.
- You owe about what the motorcycle is worth after two years.
- Note that more interest is paid in the first year.
- Note that the interest is now half of what the principal payments are.

BEST LOAN

Three-year loan for $12,650 with $2,000 down payment at 7.79 percent interest

	MONTHLY PAYMENT	INTEREST	CAPITAL	ENDING BALANCE
1	$332.70	$69.14	$263.57	$10,386.43
2	$332.70	$67.43	$265.28	$10,121.16
3	$332.70	$65.70	$267.00	$9,854.16
4	$332.70	$63.97	$268.73	$9,585.43
5	$332.70	$62.23	$270.48	$9,314.95
6	$332.70	$60.47	$272.23	$9,042.72
7	$332.70	$58.70	$274.00	$8,768.72
8	$332.70	$56.92	$275.78	$8,492.94
9	$332.70	$55.13	$277.57	$8,215.38
10	$332.70	$53.33	$279.37	$7,936.01
11	$332.70	$51.52	$281.18	$7,654.82
12	$332.70	$49.69	$283.01	$7,371.81
13	$332.70	$47.86	$284.85	$7,086.97
14	$332.70	$46.01	$286.70	$6,800.27
15	$332.70	$44.15	$288.56	$6,511.71
16	$332.70	$42.27	$290.43	$6,221.29
17	$332.70	$40.39	$292.32	$5,928.97
18	$332.70	$38.49	$294.21	$5,634.76
19	$332.70	$36.58	$296.12	$5,338.64
20	$332.70	$34.66	$298.04	$5,040.59
21	$332.70	$32.72	$299.98	$4,740.61
22	$332.70	$30.77	$301.93	$4,438.68
23	$332.70	$28.81	$303.89	$4,134.80
24	$332.70	$26.84	$305.86	$3,828.94
	$1,163.78			

- After two years, you have paid $1,163.78 in interest.
- Your loan never exceeds the value of your motorcycle if you were to sell it.
- Interest paid is the lowest.
- More goes to capital.

Three-year loan for $7,000 with $2,000 down payment at 7.79 percent interest

	MONTHLY PAYMENT	INTEREST	CAPITAL	ENDING BALANCE
1	$156.20	$32.46	$123.74	$4,876.26
2	$156.20	$31.66	$124.54	$4,751.72
3	$156.20	$30.85	$125.35	$4,626.37
4	$156.20	$30.03	$126.17	$4,500.20
5	$156.20	$29.21	$126.98	$4,373.22
6	$156.20	$28.39	$127.81	$4,245.41
7	$156.20	$27.56	$128.64	$4,116.77
8	$156.20	$26.72	$129.47	$3,987.30
9	$156.20	$25.88	$130.31	$3,856.98
10	$156.20	$25.04	$131.16	$3,725.82
11	$156.20	$24.19	$132.01	$3,593.81
12	$156.20	$23.33	$132.87	$3,460.94
13	$156.20	$22.47	$133.73	$3,327.21
14	$156.20	$21.60	$134.60	$3,192.62
15	$156.20	$20.73	$135.47	$3,057.14
16	$156.20	$19.85	$136.35	$2,920.79
17	$156.20	$18.96	$137.24	$2,783.55
18	$156.20	$18.07	$138.13	$2,645.43
19	$156.20	$17.17	$139.02	$2,506.40
20	$156.20	$16.27	$139.93	$2,366.47
21	$156.20	$15.36	$140.84	$2,225.64
22	$156.20	$14.45	$141.75	$2,083.89
23	$156.20	$13.53	$142.67	$1,941.22
24	$156.20	$12.60	$143.60	$1,797.62
		$546.38		

- After two years, you have paid $546.38 in interest.
- Your loan never exceeds the value of your motorcycle if you were to sell it.
- Interest paid is the lowest.
- More goes to capital.

INSURING YOUR MOTORCYCLE

I would be remiss to not mention insuring your motorcycle. This is an added cost and most likely a legal requirement. The insurance setup for a motorcycle is similar to that of your car in that you'll need to get a basic amount and consider the option of additional coverage. Figuring out how much insurance to buy takes some thought and planning. If you don't do some research, you could easily end up spending well over $100 per month, or even $200, just to ride around. Be sure to establish insurance costs when you are budgeting for a motorcycle by giving your local insurer a call.

Most motorcycle insurance is based on your age, claims history, where you live, the value of your motorcycle, and the size of its engine. Since large portions of insurance claims occur to those under the age of twenty-five, expect to pay more if you are in this category. If you are a car driver with a few points against your name, this may carry over into your motorcycle insurance. If an insurance company has several claims in the area where you live, this could also affect your cost. The more expensive the motorcycle, the more expensive the claims may be, so be prepared for your costs to go up. The engine size matters too: bigger bikes simply cost more to insure. The most efficient and cost-effective motorcycle to insure is a smaller one. Buy a 400cc or smaller, and your insurance costs should be golden.

When insuring your motorcycle, it's easy to be carried away and find yourself buying expensive coverage. Of course, you want to protect your investment, but do balance your bike's insurance with other coverage you may need. You are by far the most important asset, and your ability to be there for your family and generate income is paramount. If you have all this motorcycle coverage, but you have no idea what you'd do if you were hurt and unable to work, it's time to rethink things. Check with the company you work for and see what sort of benefits you have. If it seems inadequate, or you plain don't have it, it's time to look into individual coverage. You can ask about this coverage from any insurance broker or financial planner. Be prepared, as it might be expensive, but it is, after all, covering your greatest asset—you.

CURB YOUR SPENDING, NOT YOUR PASSION

I don't know what's more dangerous: the siren call of your dream motorcycle or the offer of a loan with appalling terms to buy it. Motorcycles are undoubtedly seductive, but they're also expensive, and those expenses can get wildly out of control depending on your excitement and involvement in your new hobby. Given the lack of control you may exercise in riding your new motorcycle, it's prudent to exercise some control where you can: namely, in the sensible financing and insuring of your bike.

CHAPTER 6

BASIC MOTORCYCLE SAFETY

Of all the locations to crash while riding a motorcycle, I'm grateful for the scene of my first crash—a track day for new riders. Riding around orange cones with no cars, gravel, or poles to contend with, I leaned my motorcycle too far into a corner. My tires gave way and my body and bike hit the ground and slid. When I stopped sliding, I just lay there uncertain if I'd hurt myself until someone rushed over to check on me. Dressed head-to-toe in leather, thankfully, I was unharmed. My bike, on the other hand, was not. It wasn't significantly damaged: $40 in parts and I was good to go.

Cosmetically, though, it was no longer perfect and pretty, as it had sustained some scratches. Still, I was glad to have learned that leaning the motorcycle that far into a bend was something I never, ever wanted to do on the road.

Undoubtedly, my first crash was a lucky one. I've since gone on to have a few more and again survived them unscathed. Motorcycles are tough. They'll handle crashes quite well and some better than others. Many motorcycle riders aren't as fortunate. Motorcycle rider deaths are twenty-seven times more common than car driver deaths, according to the Insurance Institute for Highway Safety, making this chapter on basic motorcycle safety vital. So, pay heed: what's to follow will show you how easy it is to avoid being one of those statistics.

MOTORCYCLING IS DANGEROUS

Is motorcycling dangerous? Yes. One-hundred percent. Motorcycle riding is dangerous. Indeed, every year, I watch riders on YouTube find new ways to crash their motorcycles. As dangerous as riding is, it's also exciting, thrilling, and challenging, making the risk worthwhile. The risk, however, should be a calculated one, especially as the dangers of riding a motorcycle are well known.

The first danger of motorcycle riding comes in the form of the motorcycle itself. Unlike a perfectly balanced car, when the kickstand on a bike is up, it doesn't stand on its own. It's the rider's job to keep the bike upright. Not paying attention, using the controls improperly, or over-leaning into a corner will cause the motorcycle and yourself to take a tumble.

The brakes are key in helping you not crash, but used improperly, they will cause you to crash quicker. A lot of motorcycle accidents are single vehicle accidents where the rider crashed because they hit the brakes too hard after becoming spooked by a car, animal, or an object on the road. Learning to use the brakes effectively takes time and patience.

Intersections represent another danger to motorcycle riders. According to statistics from my local insurance company, ICBC, 73 percent of the claims they receive take place at intersections. This easily makes intersections the most dangerous place to ride your motorcycle. Think about it: it's where cars, buses, and bikes cross paths, so the chances of confusion and ignorance around the rules of the road are high. With so much activity, small things can get overlooked and go unseen. And by small things, I mean you, the motorcycle rider.

Corners come a close second to the intersection for dangerous places for motorcycles to be. That's because the motorcycle rider's own impulse is to fixate on where they don't want to go. Known as target fixation, targets can come in the form of potholes, gravel, oncoming traffic, etc. Know that wherever you look while on a bike is where the bike will go. The advice then is to look where you want to go. In the countless conversations I've had with interesting and noteworthy riders, their biggest tip for riding safe and fast was looking where you want to go. Looking farther down the road or track, they echo, is key to a safe line through a corner, with your peripheral vision providing you with all the information you need to know.

Speed variance is another motorcycle hazard. When a motorcycle or vehicle is going faster or slower than other traffic, it's tough for drivers around them to observe, interpret, and react to any hazards present. In the case of excessive speed, a motorcycle rider's reaction time is considerably compromised. What's more, drivers just can't react effectively around speeding motorcyclists. They just don't know what to expect. Bottom line: be predictable and go with the flow of traffic, like a twig amongst the shoulders of a mighty stream.

Finally, as with driving, riding a motorcycle under the influence of alcohol is a surefire way to invite danger. Studies show that 33 percent of riders killed in motorcycle crashes have been drinking. Only one-third of those riders had a blood alcohol concentration above the legal limits. The rest had only a few drinks in their systems, which was enough to impair their riding skills. Riding a motorcycle safely is a demanding and complex task. It requires careful observation of an ever-changing environment and quick and skillful decisions—none of which can be safely done with alcohol in the bloodstream. Even if you are legally allowed to drive or ride with a small amount of alcohol in your system, don't do it.

MINIMIZING DANGERS: THE BASICS

As dire as these dangers sound, providing your crash isn't fatal, crashing can be a good thing, as it helps you learn your limits. Ideally, if you crash, it will be in the safe and controlled environment of a motorcycle training school, advanced school, or track day. If your crash takes place in other environments, there are still a number of precautions you can take to increase your odds of surviving.

Improving your understanding of your bike and how to perform key emergency maneuvers on it is a good place to start. Emergency stops are an important maneuver to practice both when you're driving in a straight line and while taking a corner. Consider what you'd do if you were riding down a road and a raccoon ran out in front of you, or worse, a child. What if you took a corner badly and didn't know how to lean or corner your motorcycle out of it? In both instances, you'd need to make snap decisions. To do so, you need to be genuinely comfortable with the motorcycle you're riding and what to do on it from how much pressure to apply to its brakes, to taking a safer line, or just riding through.

Even if you are a perfect rider, crashes still happen. While well covered in Chapter 3, it bears repeating—donning head-to-toe protective clothing seriously reduces the risk of death, head, or face trauma and soft tissue injuries. I've been on a couple of rides where the riders were in crashes so ferocious they required helicopter medical evacuation. It's only because they were wearing full gear that they were able to survive, and after a recovery period, return to riding the next season. Couple protective clothing with avoiding alcohol and regulating your speed to the flow of traffic, and you've immediately increased your chances of not meeting your end on a motorcycle.

On the topic of controlling things, be sure your bike is in excellent condition. Of primary importance is the state of your tires, as they are the point of contact between your motorcycle and the road. As discussed in Chapter 5, motorcycle tires are round and made of a very soft compound, which when subject to varying temperatures can warp, wear, and become misshapen. Be sure to check your tires regularly, as well as your oil. If in doubt, get a second opinion from a mechanic or someone with a good set of eyes and an even better understanding of bikes. You'll want to find problems in the safety of your driveway or mechanic versus somewhere in the middle of nowhere.

MINIMIZING DANGERS: KNOWLEDGE IS SAFETY

The time of day matters when you ride your motorcycle, and it can be a simple thing to tweak to keep you safe. The safest time to ride a motorcycle is between 9:00 a.m. and 12:00 p.m. There are less drunk people on the road, and your energy levels are at their highest, ensuring your reaction time is at its best. It follows that the worst time to ride a motorcycle is between 3:00 p.m. and 3:00 a.m. During this period, you're exposed to rush hour traffic, the setting sun in your eyes, or no sun at all, and those driving over the alcohol limit—all hazardous things you have little or no control over.

You might well wonder if you should even ride at night. Yes, is the answer: it's perfectly safe. You will, however, have to be more aware of the dangers, such as not seeing the road as clearly, extra glare from traffic, colder temperatures, more animals on the road, and your invisibility. The trick is to keep your speed reasonable. If you ride too fast, your headlight will not shine far enough down the road. You can also wear a Hi-Viz vest or jacket, or consider buying a cool LED lighting kit (called LightMode) for your helmet. All these things will minimize the dangers and help keep you visible.

The time of day matters and the day of the week, too. Know that on weekends and holidays, there are more motorcycle accidents. If you do find yourself riding on these days, exercise more caution. Better yet, avoid holiday weekends for motorcycle rides altogether. My motorcycle buddies and I like to plan rides around long weekends and some of the best, quietest rides have been in September; it's when everyone is done taking holidays, and the mountains are nice and quiet for us.

Age plays a factor in motorcycling, as well as time. Every motorcycle class I teach has a wide spectrum of new riders of all ages. If you are a male under the age of thirty who is going to ride a super sport motorcycle, statistically speaking, you are in the highest risk category. This doesn't mean you'll crash; it just means you must exercise the greatest degree of discipline and safety. The over-forty-rider crowd is the largest group, so naturally, it has the most amount of rider crashes. Reaction time and recovery time are longer the older we get, so if you find yourself in this category, you, too, need greater discipline and safety. Since women are a much smaller percentage of riders, there isn't enough data to suggest they are safer riders. Anecdotally speaking, however, it seems there is never a shortage of women riders out there. In any of the group rides I have been on, it has mostly been the guys crashing. Women, it seems, are far better at being disciplined and keeping the speed reasonable.

SOME GOOD NEWS

From 2005 to 2014, the amount of motorcyclists on the road has increased by 35 percent. Curiously, the number of fatalities did not, while injuries only increased by 6 percent. I'd like to hope rider education, motorcycle gear, safety, and technology are changing the stats, making it altogether safer to ride motorcycles.

Here are more stats proving this: Equity Red Star, a leading insurer, found a motorcyclist that regularly drives a car is a safer driver. They are apparently 23 percent less likely on average to make a claim on their car policy. They are also 20 percent less likely to make a bodily injury claim. Simply put: as riders, we accept more risk in our lives riding motorcycles, but we actually decrease our risk of a car crash.

One last thing: since ABS was first introduced in 1988, it has now, thankfully, become more mainstream. As such, ABS is now on the minds of insurers, and their statistics are showing upturns. A motorcycle with ABS is less likely to be in a fatal crash, for instance. Collision claims with ABS-equipped motorcycles meanwhile are 23 percent less and rider injuries 34 percent less. ABS works, but it is not a guarantee. Treat ABS as an insurance policy if you hit the brakes too hard for the surface you are braking on. In the meantime, learn how to slow down your motorcycle without it.

HOW I'VE STAYED SAFE ALL THESE YEARS

As a riding instructor, you'd expect me to know more than most about keeping safe on my bike. And you'd be right. It's knowledge, not a random streak of luck that has kept me safe. With what society and the statistics say about motorcycling, though, it still may seem a little unfathomable. It may seem like I won the lottery of motorcycle riding. The thing is, it's not just me who has had a long, safe experience of riding bikes—many motorcyclists have. Sure, us lucky ones have had some bumps along the way, but if you've read this far, you'll know most of them can be avoided. But, if you're still wondering what my secrets are, allow me to share them.

First, I've ridden within my limits, most of the time. When I was a new rider, I did exceed them more often than I should, but thankfully my smaller motorcycle kept me out of extreme danger, more than a larger bike would have. It also helps that I have a healthy sense of self-preservation, too.

From day one on a motorcycle, I wore All The Gear, All The Time. That point alone is so important we motorcycle instructors have an acronym for it: ATGATT. Riding fully geared-up meant I knew that if I did fall, I was giving myself the best odds of walking away, simply with a great story. The pavement is not forgiving, so I've always been clear that I'd rather crash at high speed with gear than at low speed with no gear.

I don't drink and ride. Period. Alcohol has its place and it's at the end of a motorcycle ride.

I've kept learning and taking additional motorcycle courses. During the riding season, I will take some form of training on the track or through other programs. The more additional training I take, the safer it makes me for the street. Crashing in a controlled environment is far safer than outside in the real world.

I'll be honest: keeping the speed reasonable is a never-ending challenge on any motorcycle. The legal speed limits seem slow even with what entry-level motorcycles are capable of. I have always kept the speed reasonable, but I do ride at a spirited pace. In my years of riding, it has earned me very, very few speeding tickets. I keep the speed reasonable because I get my speed fix out on the track. I have my outlet for it, so it's much easier to relax and enjoy the ride.

Keeping yourself in check is one thing; resisting peer pressure is another. It's easy to get caught up in a group ride where riders are going way too fast. While it's human nature to want to keep up and be part of the group, I've always known if I do this, I'm placing myself at immense risk. My advice: ease up. Get a riding buddy so both of you can watch out for each other. If the riding group you are with just takes off, they're not worth it. A great riding group waits for everyone and checks to make sure everyone is accounted for. My riding group is made up of respectful riders; we check in with each other, and we know to ride our own ride. If you're going to be riding in groups, I suggest you find the same.

Helping others on the road has also brought me good karma. As motorcyclists, we are the minority on the road. Anytime a rider needs help, I always do what I can. I have benefited more from riders helping me out, and of course, I want to pay it forward. If you see a rider on the side of the road, give them the thumbs-up to see if they're okay. They may just need someone to chat with while the tow truck comes to get them.

IT'S NOT WHEN BUT HOW

Bikes are simple: two wheels and a motor. But as with everything in life, that simplicity comes at a price. Horribly exposed to other vehicles and poor roads with just your gear and helmet for protection, motorcycle riding is as dangerous a pastime as it gets. Consequently, crashes are part of riding a bike. It could happen right away, it may not happen for years, but a crash will happen to you. Knowing this, be a smart rider and minimize unavoidable dangers through safe driving, good motorcycle maintenance, and calculated routes.

BASIC RIDING
TECHNIQUES

A mere two years into riding, I found myself in a group of riders who wanted to do big rides. My riding skills were tested constantly, but the ultimate test came when twelve of us set out to ride from British Colombia to Utah and Arizona, then back through California to home.

Up until that point, I had managed to stay within my limits with the group, but on this trip, I was unprepared for so much. First, there were the sights and smells of countless new places. Imagine an ultra white plain of salt so flat you can see for miles, the spectacular colors of Zion National Park and cruising into the dazzling lights of Las Vegas. I was blind sighted by so much beauty. The technical roads I had to ride to reach these wonders also challenged me. I had no choice but to keep a close eye on the riders better than me and work hard to copy their skills one mile at a time.

Known as the Epic Trip, this adventure is still one of my greatest, despite its difficulties. This is motorcycle riding as I know it. As a motorcycle instructor, there is nothing that I enjoy more than seeing my students have safe experiences on their motorcycle, but above all, fun ones. So, with safety wrapped up, let's survey the basic riding techniques you'll need to take to the road.

HOW RIDING A MOTORCYCLE IS DIFFERENT FROM A CAR

It's an obvious thing to say, but a worthwhile point to reiterate: riding a motorcycle is nothing like driving a car. Even if you're the driver of a fast sports car, it does nothing to help you ride a motorcycle. In addition to the basic fact that you are exposed to the world on your motorcycle, it is also simply just you, whatever motorcycle gear you're wearing, and your motorcycle. But there are greater differences, and they're worth reviewing.

The first notable difference is the weight of a motorcycle.

With a car, you're oblivious to its size, but hop on a bike, and you'll immediately notice how heavy it is. Couple this with the fact you're on two round wheels, and balance will be your first challenge to meet. Learning how to prevent your bike from falling over when it's not on its kickstand comes with practice.

Two wheels make slow speed maneuvers challenging. Do not be in a hurry to go fast. Riding a motorcycle slowly is an essential skill to learn. You may only ride slowly 5 percent to 10 percent of the time, but if you almost drop your motorcycle every time you're in a gas station, parking lot, or heavy traffic, it's going to get expensive. You might hurt yourself and no one will want to ride with you.

Unlike a car, and more like a bicycle, a motorcycle doesn't have a steering wheel. The next difference you'll swiftly have to grow accustomed to is steering with handlebars. At slower speeds, you'll turn your handlebars in the direction you wish to go: left to go left and right to go right. Anything over around twenty-five kilometers/fifteen miles, however, and you'll need to learn to move the handlebars in the opposite direction. This is called counter-steering and it's very intuitive. If you've ever ridden a bicycle at a higher speed, you have already experienced counter-steering. If this seems crazy and you just can't wrap your head around it, wait until you get on your motorcycle. I remember my first training course and experimenting with counter-steering. I thought I was going to crash but it actually felt very natural and right.

One thing intuition won't help you with, however, is visibility. A motorcycle has just one headlight, unlike a car that has two. The same goes for taillights: you're stuck with one, while a car gets three lights to show that the vehicle is slowing down. When you just have one light, it's harder for other vehicles to determine where exactly that one light is and how fast it's going. That's if they see you at all, as it's easy to blend in to the traffic you are in. You can put additional lights on the front and back of motorcycles, which will help, but don't rely on them. As ever, care and vigilance on your behalf are key.

A headlight isn't the only thing a motorcycle is missing: it also possesses no reverse gear. Reversing your bike is a manual operation requiring some physical effort to pull the bike back. You can pull the motorcycle back while it's running, or you can turn the bike off, put it into neutral, and back the motorcycle up while it's not running. The safer of the two options is the latter. If you back the bike up while it's in gear, and you let the clutch out by accident, or rev the engine, the motorcycle could shoot forward unexpectedly.

Speaking of the unexpected, another big difference between motorcycles and cars is the signals: motorcycle signals are often not self-cancelling. Only a few motorcycles have self-canceling signals—Harley Davidsons and high-end BMWs among them. Signals on a motorcycle will stay on until you turn them off. Should you forget and ride around with signals blinking, it's obviously hazardous, as it leaves other vehicles confused about your intentions. If you ever find yourself leaving your signals on, use your hand signals. Those have built in self-canceling features.

Hazards, of course, are plenty on a motorcycle, including the otherwise harmless weather. On a motorcycle, you're completely exposed to the elements, and while it's easy to stay warm, it's much harder to stay cool. Moreover, on a motorcycle, there's no sun visor, so without a helmet with a dark enough visor, you can spend much of the ride squinting. Squinting obscures your field of vision and places you at great risk. It's worth mentioning that dawn and dusk are particularly dangerous times to ride a motorcycle. The low-lying sun causes everyone's visibility to be much lower, especially motorcyclists. Be very careful around this time of day—the motorists coming toward you could be blinded by the sun and not see you at all.

Certainly, what you don't want to go unseen is the state of your tires, as a motorcycle, unlike a car, doesn't run on flat tires and doesn't have a spare one. As a temporary solution, it's wise to carry a small tire repair kit and a small hand pump. Your local automotive store will carry the kit, and bicycle shops have very small and efficient hand pumps. These will offer you a good chance of fixing the tire if you are stuck in the middle of nowhere. Plugging a tire is not a guaranteed solution. Most likely, it will work, and you could very well run that tire until it wears out, but be sure to get it checked when you get home and swap out the tire for a new one that's not compromised.

The differences between a motorcycle and a car don't stop with physical attributes but extend to operation. While they both start with a key, what a motorcycle asks your hands and feet to do are vastly different. Your left hand, for instance, will operate the clutch lever. You'll pull this lever in to shift gears and to come to a stop. Your left thumb will operate the signals, horn, and high beam. Your right hand takes care of the throttle with a twist of the grip. It doesn't take much to really get the engine going; you'll need a steady and controlled hand. You operate the front brakes with a lever controlled by your right hand. Like the throttle, it requires a steady and controlled hand. You'll spend a lot of time, incidentally, learning to use the brakes properly. Your right thumb, meanwhile, will operate the kill switch and the starter button. Your right foot operates the rear brake. Just the tips of your toes, in fact, as the rear brake can be quite sensitive. If you press down on it too hard, the rear tire might lock up and/or your ABS will be triggered.

Still with me? Good. Now, on to your left foot. Your left foot, actually your left toes, shift the gears, clicking up and down through them. First gear is at the bottom, and then above that is neutral. Past neutral is second, third, fourth, fifth, and sixth gear. It should be noted that neutral is not a gear; in much the same way that Pluto is not a planet. Neutral is just a big space between first and second gear. Learning to shift gears on a motorcycle takes practice. Riding a motorcycle is about feel, so, too, is knowing exactly when you should shift gears. If you've never shifted gears in a car, that is just fine. It's easier to learn how to shift gears on a motorcycle. One thing's for sure: as you come to a stop, always tap down on the shift a few extra times to ensure you are in first gear, as you may need to move out of the way in a hurry. You'll be ready for this eventuality if you're in first.

HOW TO GET ON AND START A MOTORCYCLE

A motorcycle is not a car—this much now should be clear. With a little know-how and a lot of practice, however, you can be riding confidently on two wheels, and it starts with how to get on the bike.

It's advisable to approach your motorcycle from the left-hand side (the same side as the kickstand). Before settling fully into your seat, run through a standard pre-ride check to ensure your motorcycle is fit for riding. This is something I teach all my students to do before they start the engine on their bikes and make a purchase on one. In motorcycle courses, the check is known by the acronym TCLOCK. T stands for tires. Check the condition, wear, pounds per square inch and any damage to them. C is for controls. Make sure the handlebars turn left and right freely, the brake and clutch levers work, and check the rear brake and shifter: in short, anything operated by your hands and feet. Up next is L. L is for lights: your headlights, signals, and brake lights. O is for Oil: just make sure you have enough. Most bikes have a tiny sight window, which shows you if the oil is at the right level. Follow this up with C. C stands for chassis and chain. Check for any missing bolts, fluids leaking, and the condition of the chain. The chain should be clean, well-lubricated, and not too loose. Finally, there's K for kickstand. More on that below.

Put your hands on the handlebars, check over your shoulder for obstacles and swing your right leg over the seat. Now you can seat yourself comfortably. While the seat itself won't move, check that your arms are on the handlebars in a relaxed fashion and your upper body isn't stiff. In fact, treat your motorcycle like you would a dance partner. From sitting, to riding, and stopping, you want to be at one with your bike, riding it smoothly and gently.

Now seated, it's time to introduce KNIFEBC. This is an important acronym describing the series of steps to take to start the motorcycle. K stands for kickstand. If you leave your kickstand down, the motorcycle will shut down if you try to put it into gear. It's a safety measure to ensure you don't ride away with the kickstand down. If you did, turns could get a little too exciting. On to N: N stands for neutral. To check if you're in neutral gear, simply roll the motorcycle forward and backwards. Starting the motorcycle in neutral is a good thing, as it is easier on the battery. Next comes I for ignition. Pop the key in the ignition and turn it to ON. All the lights and electronics should come to life. Now check the fuel (F) and make sure you have enough. Your fuel gauge will tell you this, or if your bike does not have one, just open the gas cap and look. E follows F and should remind you to ensure the engine kill switch is not engaged. The engine kill switch prevents the motorcycle from starting or turns off the engine in the case of an emergency, while still leaving the electronics on. You'll want to squeeze the brakes on now—that would be B—so the bike doesn't roll away when you start it. Front or rear brake is fine. Finally, pull your clutch (C) in and then find the start button. Press the start button as if you were ringing a doorbell, and the bike should come to life.

HOW TO TACKLE LANES, CORNERING, BRAKING, AND MORE

You're seated, and your motorcycle engine is running, but before you leave the safety of the stationary position, it's worth re-visiting the riding skills both new and experienced riders struggle with.

First up, there's lane positioning. Your motorcycle is small and nimble. You have plenty of room to move around in your lane, so use this to your advantage. Always be pro-active and dominant. Position yourself on the road, so you've got a bubble of space around you. This will give you options should you need to get out of the way. Vehicles and trucks may not have the right of way, but they have the right of weight. Moreover, planting yourself visibly and dominantly in traffic will earn you respect. If you're riding very slowly while gripping the shoulder of the road, other vehicles will drive dangerously and disrespectfully past you, believing you're nothing more than a cyclist.

As a motorcycle rider, know that the entire lane is legally yours, and you're not obliged to hug the side of the lane closest to the shoulder. Lane positions are marked by numbers. Number one is the left portion of the lane. Number two is the middle, and lane position three is the right-hand side. Wherever you choose to position yourself within the lane, be sure to choose the safest position—the one that gives you the largest amount of space between you and your greatest threat. You'll also want to consider a lane position that's going to allow you to maintain dominance and presence while riding in traffic.

Since you're riding in an ever-changing flow of vehicles, lane positioning is an art and not a science. Schools and riders always talk in length about this, and their talk is likely to be highly opinionated. Listen to other people's opinions, but make up your own. While we're talking opinions and subjectivity, there are certain situations where it's possible to be prescriptive. Take intersections, for example. It doesn't matter how busy the intersection is, you are the most vulnerable vehicle in it. Drop your speed, get into the most visible lane, and when the light is green, check left and right to ensure everyone is doing what they should be doing. If you ignore everything and everyone and only rely on the green light, something will be missed and that something is likely to be you. If everything is fairly clear at the intersection, lane position one is fine. If there's traffic in the oncoming lane waiting to turn left, and there's a chance they'll turn in front of you without notice, lane position three is wisest.

Hills can be as tricky as intersections, given your visibility is compromised by the crest of the hill. Occupying lane position three is best in these circumstances, so if a vehicle does come over the hill and is drifting onto your side of the road, you're in the safest position possible.

One of the most difficult things to do on a motorcycle is turning a corner. Anyone can ride along in a straight line, but hit that first tight corner, and you can quickly separate the accomplished from the less accomplished rider. The basic advice with corners is to look where you want to go. If you're riding at an appropriate speed, the bike should safely follow. More specifically, as you approach a corner, slow down and assess how tight and long the corner is, plus whether there are any changes to the road elevation or surface. Your observations should go on to inform your speed and gear selection. Ideally, all your braking and gear changes should take place before you enter the corner, as these actions affect the motorcycle.

As for lane position, you'll want to try to take the straightest line through the corner. This might look like entering from the far side of the corner, tightening up on the inside and exiting on the far side. Couple your route through the corner with good body positioning. If you're turning left, for example, move your head and shoulders, and maybe even your torso and knee, toward the corner to help the bike take it, remembering to keep your eyes on where you want to go. When you use your body, the tires don't have to lean as much, which means more traction on the road. Proper body positioning matters on all types of motorcycles but does vary with the bike. With sports bikes, body positioning is very complex and detailed. With cruisers, it does not matter as much. Dirt bikes have a very different approach to body positioning. Whatever you ride, learn the best body positioning for it. It will keep you safe and smooth through those corners, so you can speed up and shift up the gears to exit cleanly.

Braking is an absolute no-no in a corner, but it's challenging at any time. If you are curious about why motorcycles cannot brake on a corner, visit YouTube and look up the channel, Rnickeymouse. YouTube is a fantastic resource, more broadly, on what not to do on a motorcycle. But when it comes to braking, it spectacularly illustrates one of the difficulties of braking: the fact that using your brakes causes the bike's weight distribution to change, which can destabilize it and send you straight to the ground. When you use the brakes, the motorcycle should be upright and straight, and you should be looking forward. Knowing how much pressure to apply to the brakes on the surface you are riding is another big challenge. While every bike brakes differently, and you'll have to experiment with your own, ideally, you'll want to start squeezing the brake lever slowly, and when it starts to take hold, apply greater pressure. When you're coming to a stop, get off the throttle, pull in the clutch and tap down the gears gently and smoothly until the whole action combined brings you to a solid stop.

PRACTICE, PRACTICE, PRACTICE

In the safety of my motorcycle school's parking lot, before my students ever turn on the ignition, I request they sit on a motorcycle and receive a big push forward. With the momentum generated by the push, the student rolls forward and gains an immediate sense of the balance and operation required to ride a bike. It's a quiet introduction to motorcycle riding, but it's usually enough to alert them, as hopefully this chapter has shown you, just how hard it is to stay safe on a motorcycle without mastering basic riding techniques. Take the time to learn the in's and out's of your motorcycle, while practicing lane position, cornering, and braking. Before long you, too, will be off on your own two-wheel adventures.

CHAPTER 8

BASIC MECHANICS AND MAINTENANCE

It was the start of a five-day motorcycle trip, and I was an hour away from home when it happened. One minute, I was dreaming of the roads I'd soon encounter, and in the next moment, my motorcycle lost all power. I coasted to the side of the road, jumped off my bike and noticed engine oil leaking out. I took a closer look and saw that my chain no longer existed. It had snapped and flown off, blowing a hole in my engine casing out of which the oil leaked. I was now stranded, but at least I was alive. Had the chain snapped slightly higher, it could have hit my left foot, and the bike wouldn't have been the only thing that needed major repair.

Motorcycles are tough, reliable forms of transport making it easy to overlook general maintenance until it's too late. I learned the hard way, so you don't have to. Look after your bike and it will look after you. Don't think you have to be a mechanic to maintain your motorcycle. It doesn't take much knowledge or effort to do the minimum, and this chapter is going to show you how.

THE BASICS OF MOTORCYCLE MAINTENANCE

Like cars, computers, and pretty much every other large ticket item, a motorcycle comes with an owner's manual. With information on everything you'll need to keep your specific motorcycle in tiptop shape, your manual should be your first port of call when you have questions about your bike's maintenance. If your motorcycle didn't come with a manual, you can get them free online or order a replacement at minimal cost from a motorcycle dealer. Next to a reliable mechanic, your motorcycle owner's manual is a rider's best friend.

Online forums and online rider groups can also be an excellent source of information. If you put the name of your motorcycle followed by the word discussion or forum into your search engine, you'll find websites dedicated to your motorcycle. The forums will be full of riders who own the same motorcycle you do, so you'll be able to see what they are experiencing with your motorcycle, good and bad. This is the Internet, so while you can ask questions of people, not all information and opinions you receive will be accurate or nice.

As constant a source of information as these two avenues are, the following is a useful checklist of things you'll need to keep an eye on, irrespective of the brand of your bike. It starts with your motorcycle's chain.

Located at your rear tire. Typically on the left side of your bike, is your motorcycle chain. Turn your back wheel or roll your bike forward, and you'll see how the chain rolls the rear tire. The chain is the part of the bike that propels you forward. The chain is directly connected to the engine, so every time you twist the throttle, the chain pulls faster and harder. Given its critical function, the motorcycle chain is under an immense amount of stress every time you ride. If your chain isn't clean and regularly lubricated, it can dry out and seize, or worse, as I discovered, break. As a good rule of thumb, you should be putting chain lubricant on it every 1,000 kilometers, or 600 miles (more frequently if you often ride in rain). If it's really dry, rusted, and kinked, it should be replaced immediately. Look out also for how tight or loose the chain is.

To check your chain to see how tight or loose it is, take your motorcycle key, and slide it under the chain. The best place to do this is halfway between the rear tire and engine where it would have the most amount of slack. See how much the chain moves up or down with the key. If you can't move the chain up at all, then your chain is likely too tight. If it moves up more than two inches, it's probably too loose. To tighten the chain, check your motorcycle manual. It's an easy job, but if it's your first time, buddy up with someone and tackle this job together. YouTube works, if your friend's busy.

As a chain ages, it naturally stretches and becomes loose, eventually affecting the responsiveness of your throttle. Your motorcycle chain will last over 20,000 kilometers (12,500 miles) if you take care of it. If you don't, it may not last more than 5,000 kilometers (3,000 miles). To replace a motorcycle chain, sprockets, and the labor to install it could cost $250-$400. Putting in the minimal effort to take care of your chain will undoubtedly save you money and keep you safe.

Oil is the blood of the motorcycle, so changing your motorcycle's oil every 5,000 kilometers (3,000 miles) is another general maintenance act that will keep your bike riding well. Remember to use oil made for a motorcycle, not a car. Car oil will wreck your motorcycle's clutch. To change the oil, locate the large drain bolt at the bottom of the motorcycle. Loosen the bolt and catch the escaping oil in a pan before putting the bolt back in. It's recommended that you change the crush washer on the drain bolt. Before adding fresh oil, it's also a good idea to check the condition of your oil filter and replace it. With a funnel, pour the fresh oil in while looking at the oil window, often contained on the side engine. Make sure the motorcycle is upright when checking the oil level. When the oil window shows two-thirds full, then your bike has adequate oil. You may want to take this messy job to a mechanic, as it won't cost much, and they'll dispose of the used oil properly.

Of equal importance to changing your bike's oil is the condition of your tires. As covered, tires need to be replaced about every five years if you don't ride very often. As tires age, the compounds in them harden, meaning less traction and, therefore, much less safety. To check the age of your tires, look for their date stamp, which is typically, a four-digit code. A code that reads 3913, for example, means the tire was made in the 39th week of 2013. If it's looking faint, don't hesitate to get your tires changed right away. If you can't locate your date stamp, you can look at the general condition of your tires' tread. Trying to push your tires to the very end of their life is dangerous. Motorcycle tires last as little as 5,000-15,000 kilometers (3,000-9,000 miles) depending on how you ride and take care of them.

Speaking of tires, be sure to keep an eye on your tire pressure.

Consult your motorcycle owner's manual to see how much air pressure is required in both your front and rear tires, as the amount will be different. Alternatively, motorcycle forums tend to post such information, but be aware of any recommendations you find, because they will be highly subjective. Be sure to check your air pressure before you ride when your tires are cold. As hot air expands, don't check your tires after a ride, as a warmer tire will give you a different PSI reading. If you have a bicycle pump, that will do for topping up the air in your tires. Most bicycle pumps have a PSI gauge on them so it makes it easy to put the right amount of air in them. If you're out riding and caught with soft tires, a gas station air compressor will work, but they are a challenge to work with. If you're lazy with any of this, be aware you're risking your safety. Under-inflated tires will feel soft and spongy and won't react properly when maneuvering quickly. Tires that are over inflated, meanwhile, will feel rock hard and provide less traction.

It's important that you also ride on a tire that is designed for your type of riding. If you ride sports bikes with a racetrack specific tire and only ride on city streets, the tire will never heat up enough. A tire needs to be warm or hot to provide the maximum level of traction. A less aggressive tire would be better if your riding consists of city streets with the occasional weekend ride into the mountains. If your riding is only commuting, then a commuting tire will do. Brands such as

Michelin, Pirelli, Metzler, Dunlop, and Bridgestone all have various types of tires for your style of riding. With any tires, the hotter they are from riding, the more traction they provide. As such, always take it easy for your first part of the ride. Once the tires heat up, you can rely on them more. On really cold days, your tires may never heat up, so be careful.

Holding the front tire in place are two cylinders known as the fork tubes. The fork tubes manage suspension by absorbing the bumps in the road. Having motorcycle suspension properly adjusted can make a night and day difference to how the motorcycle rides. If your motorcycle isn't riding as smoothly as you'd like, look at your bike's manual for suspension tweaks, which are best done by a mechanic or a motorcycle suspension specialist. As for the rear suspension, most motorcycles do not have advanced suspensions, so you can certainly do an adjustment of the rear shock yourself. The more suspension adjustments your bike needs is more of a reason you should see a specialist about it. It really does make the motorcycle ride beautifully.

The health of your brakes should be, understandably, high on your maintenance list. Here are two things to consider: brake fluid and brake pads. Your front and rear brakes both possess a brake fluid reservoir and this needs to be topped up or changed. How often is determined by how much you ride. Brake fluid can absorb moisture over time, so it needs to be changed in order to ensure that it retains its properties. It's easy to keep an eye on your brake fluid levels as the reservoir has a little window, the size of a dime, and is typically located between the ignition and the right handlebar. Brake fluid works in conjunction with the brake pads and rotors to slow the bike down. To check the state of your brake pads, shine a flashlight on the clamp attached to the rotor, which contains the pads. If the pads are around half a centimeter (0.2 inches), they are still safe, but if they're thinner and cracked, replace these as soon as possible. Replacing the pads isn't difficult, but since your braking performance can be deeply affected by installing them incorrectly, it's best to take this job to a mechanic at the very least to check you've done the work correctly.

There's certainly oil and fluid aplenty you need to administer to your bike, and the final one on the list is motorcycle coolant. The cooling system in your bike is important, because it stops your engine from overheating and possibly being destroyed. Check it every so often and especially in very hot weather. If your bike starts leaking coolant in great pools of green liquid, be sure to take it to a mechanic right away. This is a serious problem and needs to be addressed.

You'd think the clutch on a motorcycle would be just as testy as it is on a stick-shift car, although surprisingly, it's not. The clutch can stand up to a lot of abuse as it sits in oil and is well lubricated. This means you can take your clutch through its various friction points and it shouldn't burn out. A clutch in a car, meanwhile, is a dry clutch and does not sit in oil, so it can burn easily. That's not to say you won't have to replace your clutch one day (and you'll know when, since the clutch simply won't be as responsive). To check the condition of your clutch cable, pull the clutch lever in. At the base of the lever, you should be able to see a small cable. If it looks like it's frayed, it should be replaced.

Your clutch may need adjustment as well. Sometimes a clutch does not engage when you pull it in or it's always engaged. The metal wheel just past the base of the lever can be loosened, and there you'll find another smaller cylinder that will bring the clutch cable in or out. This is a simple adjustment that can be made by anyone. Check out YouTube if you're in any doubt as to how it's done and keep in mind if you improperly adjust your clutch, you can damage it.

Occasionally, your throttle may require maintenance, too. As you pull the throttle, you open a valve that allows more air and fuel to enter the engine, and this provides power to the bike. If your throttle refuses to snap back when turned, your throttle cable could be faulty. To mend it, have a look to see if the grip is rubbing up against anything that might prevent it from snapping back into position. If it is, you may just need to twist the grip away from the problem or loosen

oar end. If you cannot fix a throttle problem quickly, it's
t to take it to a mechanic.

hough small, your motorcycle's lights and signals are
orthy of your attention. Powered by bulbs, these will need
be replaced. The process is much the same as changing
ulbs in a house. Be sure to look at your motorcycle owner's
manual for exactly what size and style of bulb your bike
requires. Tiny hands will help with the job. If your motorcycle
has LED signals and lights, however, you may never have to
worry about them burning out.

It's important to know headlights vary across all motorcycles,
but most motorcycles just have one headlight. Some motorcycles have two headlights but only one lights up. You may
wonder if the unlit one is burnt out, but this is not the case.
One headlight is for the low beam and the other is for the
high beam; they don't stay on at the same time. Electrical
charging systems are weaker on motorcycles, since they are
smaller, which means having two headlights on at all times
is too taxing on the system. If you like HID or any brighter,
intense headlights, some motorcycles do come equipped
with them. Many, though, are installed by the rider. While
these do provide a brighter light, there are pros and cons.
The obvious pro is you will see more in front of you. The con,
however, is your eyes will adjust to a brighter light and you
won't be able to see beyond that beam of light particularly

well. To give you a point of comparison: a traditional headlight is dimmer, but outside the beam of light, you will be able to see an animal or another hazard easily. Adding low voltage LED auxiliary lights at a lower point on the motorcycle might be a better option for visibility.

If you're having trouble with your bike and haven't found the culprit, it could be that a fuse has blown. Fuses are placed differently on every motorcycle, so check your manual for location. Changing the fuse is as easy as looking in the middle of the fuse at the two thin pieces of metal. If the fuse has blown, the metal will be broken and black. Simply replace the fuse with a new one. There might be spares in the fuse case; if not, carry some spares. The act of replacing a fuse is similar to pulling a piece of toast from a toaster.

Finally, keep an eye out for your bike's battery. If you're not using your bike regularly, the battery will drain itself. A motorcycle battery will last five years if you use your bike regularly and the battery is constantly full. But if your battery is constantly being drained, and you have to recharge it, the battery's life will be much shorter. Every motorcyclist should own a battery tender. When plugged in, they keep the motor-cycle battery charged at all times. You can install a simple cable, so plugging the battery tender into your motorcycle is easy. New batteries cost around $100. At around $50, a battery tender is the cheaper of the two options.

HOW TO FIX THE BIKE ON THE ROAD

No one wants to be stuck on the side of the road fixing any of the problems I just listed. Still, if your bike does come undone while you're out riding, you'll be grateful you've carried a basic tool kit. Most bikes come with such a thing and will contain a screwdriver, wrenches, pliers, Allen keys, plus spare bolts and screws. Throw a tire plug and repair kit in there and this should be good enough to deal with minor issues. Be sure to carry money for a tow truck in case you're faced with larger problems.

Speaking of tow trucks, it's wise to sign up for a roadside assistance program, as the cost of towing a motorcycle is more expensive than a car, particularly if you need to be rescued from remote roads. I was once 200 kilometers (100 miles) from home at the start of a five-day road trip when my motorcycle lost all power. I coasted unhappily down the hill to a stop. My motorcycle had electrical issues, which were made worse by my heated grips and jacket that drew more electrical current. The bike clearly needed major electrical work and new parts, so I called my roadside assistance (BCAA), and they had a flat deck tow truck sent to me ASAP. A twenty-foot flat deck tow truck turned up, which might have seemed overkill for my small motorcycle, but a traditional tow truck cannot safely tow a motorcycle. Flat deck tow trucks cost the earth, so my tow bill was $900. Thanks to my annual BCAA membership of about $150, I didn't pay a cent.

HOW TO STORE YOUR BIKE

Storing your motorcycle is not rocket science. It's about ensuring you do the basics like washing it well and storing it properly. When you get into the regular practice of washing your bike, you'll become observant of any new problems or damage.

Problems or damage are less likely to occur if you're storing your motorcycle safely between rides. Be sure to park your bike in a cool dry place, secured with a large chain and a heavy-duty lock. You may also want to throw a cover over it. The simple act of disguising your motorcycle will discourage theft and protect it from the elements. A motorcycle covered is out of sight and, therefore, out of mind.

If your bike has to sit for a long time, the battery may well run flat. Remove the battery or keep it charged with your battery tender. If you're storing your bike for longer than thirty days and there is gas in its tank, there's a good chance your gas will become stale and gum up the carburetors. To avoid this, pour some gas stabilizer in the tank and run it for ten minutes before storing it. This will ensure your motorcycle starts on the first try when your storage time is over. It's a good idea to also change your oil before storing your motorcycle. Dirty engine oil left sitting in a bike is never ideal.

HIT THE START BUTTON

You've taken time to learn how to ride a motorcycle and put down serious cash to buy one. As nice as it is to think you can now just hit the start button and take off on your bike whenever you like, mechanical problems do and will occur. Take good care of your bike and this is less likely to happen. Better yet, acquaint yourself with basic mechanics, and you'll be riding more often than not.

CHAPTER 9

HOW TO TRADE UP

Most likely, at this point, you've decided to fully commit to motorcycling. You probably find that time flies when you're riding and slows to a halt when you're wanting to ride. Indeed, with a few months (or a few thousand miles or kilometers) of experience, it's certain that you're itching for more.

SMALL UP-GRADES AND INVESTMENTS

Perhaps your newfound love of riding leads you to want a new bike. Or maybe you want some new gear. Before deciding what exactly will satisfy your desire for more, it's worth knowing how common this feeling is. For many, it's just that riding has become familiar and all that's needed is a new challenge. Rather than thoughtlessly dropping more cash, however, I encourage you to stop and consider if you've really ridden your current bike to its full capacity.

Have you, for instance, ridden your bike beyond city limits? If you've only taken your bike to and from work, you may want to consider a longer ride. Teaming up with a riding group for a day or weekend trip is a smart idea for a relative beginner. Be sure to do your own due diligence ahead of the ride and see what kind of roads the trip will take in. It's great to follow people, but they may take you on roads that are too advanced, like those on a mountain pass where the turns exceed the stretches. Either way, just remember to ride your own ride. Go at your own pace and bring your own map, just in case you get lost. If you can, recruit a riding buddy—someone who can look out for you while en route.

What about your riding skills? Have you nailed cornering and braking? If not, a good next step would be to upgrade them by taking an advanced motorcycle course. Such a course requires that you bring your bike along to a school where they'll put you through your paces in cornering, braking, and stopping. If you do not want to use your own motorcycle, there are courses that include the motorcycle, but they do cost more. Perfecting your skills will make the whole experience of riding a motorcycle much more enjoyable, because with more knowledge comes more confidence and safety. There is definitely a cost to advanced rider training. It could be as little as a hundred bucks or as much as $2,500. It all depends on how in depth the course gets. That said, it's very worth it, as improving your riding skills will absolutely reduce your chances of getting into accidents. Think of these courses as pennies on the dollar for what it costs if you crash on the street.

You may also wish to try a different style of riding to advance your skills. Every form of two-wheel training, whatever it is, is going to help you. While I primarily ride on the street, I found great value in taking a dirt bike course. Dirt bikes slide around more than road bikes, so getting more experience maneuvering a bike in slippery circumstances means I'm now a good deal more comfortable on my street bike should the tires slide around on an unexpectedly slippery surface.

Like other forms of clothing, motorcycle gear is similarly fashion forward. Every year, retailers take out another line, mostly with new designs and even safety features. It may be then that you can scratch your motorcycle itch with some new gear. A lighter jacket for the summer, maybe. Or something from a brand you've since fallen in love with.

When you're into motorcycling, the allure of a new motorcycle is always present. Spring is when new models hit the dealers. Typically, the dealers will have demo days where you can check out all the new motorcycles and, better yet, test ride them. Make sure you turn up in your motorcycle gear and not your sweats, however. Test rides are at the discretion of the dealer. If you want the best deal on a new motorcycle, August is when the season closeout deals begin. Go with your wits about you and your homework done. Be sure you know your budget and your riding needs for the next chapter of your motorcycle adventure.

LOUDER AND PROUDER UP-GRADES AND INVESTMENTS

When my students come by the school for a visit, either to show me their new ride or to tell me where riding has brought them, it's always very interesting. The new riders who have the most fun and are the safest have a few things in common: they buy the right motorcycle gear, start with a smaller motorcycle, ride alone and with others on a regular basis, and invest in advanced rider training instead of a new exhaust pipe. All that said, I do find that the most common new rider purchase is a custom or louder exhaust.

I confess: I do love putting a new exhaust on my bike. It looks good and sounds even better, but it does nothing to make you a better rider and the gain in power is minimal. If you're buying it because loud pipes save lives, consider that the noise it emits can help in keeping other traffic around you aware of your presence. However, it's wildly inconsistent. If you ride around thinking everyone can see you because you are loud, then disappointment or worse will soon follow. While driving in traffic, people are distracted by their smartphones, loud music, and a host of other things. Another factor to consider before pimping your bike with a new exhaust is your neighbors. They will hate your loud, obnoxious motorcycle exhaust. They will not get it. Be as respectful as you can around the neighborhood where you live and avoid excessive revving in busy areas. If you are not considerate, expect your neighbors to do nasty things to your bike. Trust me, you do not want to incur the wrath of a mother with a young infant who regularly is awakened by your motorcycle. When you are out on the open road or a racetrack, by all means, open it up!

Speaking of opening it up, or rather lighting it up, high-visibility vests, jackets, and fancy lighting kits called LightMode are a less obnoxious way of getting attention as a motorcyclist. All offer greater visibility, and better visibility means you'll catch the attention of traffic easier, especially if you ride at night. Just like with loud pipes, however, you can't rely on everyone seeing you. If anything, loud pipes and Hi-Viz clothing might give you a slight visibility edge out there, but do still ride around as if you are a silent and invisible motorcyclist. Smart riding always trumps fancy gear.

THE WAVE: DO I KNOW YOU?

Another way you might encounter being seen on the road is "the wave." You know, other motorcyclists waving to you as you ride? You might be wondering why, but that's just what motorcyclists do. It doesn't matter what we ride, if we ride two wheels, we're all motorcyclists together. If you're lucky enough to live in North America, Europe, Australia, or other highly developed countries, we ride motorcycles for fun, and this is a big part of the reason we're waving. Riding makes us ridiculously happy, and we just want to share that with other riders. You may also find that other riders and non-riders will approach you to chat. Upgrade your whole experience of riding by embracing this. Most motorcyclists are social or become social.

CONCLUSION

TWO WHEELS CAN
MOVE THE SOUL

Motorcycles! They're just two wheels and an engine, but it's surprising how much happiness they've brought into my life. I was initially attracted to them out of a sheer interest in their speed. My first motorcycle, the old and heavy 400cc Honda CB1, was thrilling to me. I was riding a motorcycle!

I soon found myself able to keep up and pass larger motorcycles, as the smaller engine forced me to learn cornering amongst other more advanced skills. My real desire, however, was for a sports bike, as my riding buddies were doing bigger trips. I still love sports bikes and sports touring motorcycles. I've owned several of them, some longer than others. The point is, whatever the size or type of motorcycle you own, you really don't know what will light you up until you own it, ride it, and work on it.

One thing's for sure, if you're anything like me, you'll find you want to buy and sell your motorcycle a lot more than your car. You may even find yourself owning multiple motorcycles. Some people have a motorcycle for every day of the week. I believe I had to start a motorcycle school to justify owning all these motorcycles and riding them all the time.

You might be surprised to read that, for me, motorcycling is not just about the bikes. Motorcycling has brought my social skills out and actually changed me as a person. My social circle has grown immensely and my now stale high school friends have become history. Through these new friendships, different opportunities have opened up for me. I started a charity project with other passionate riders and created a calendar of events, which benefited the Vancouver Burn Fund. This, in turn, delivered more opportunities, like leading demo rides. Riding a motorcycle is, you see, so much more than just riding—it opens doors.

Of course, riding hasn't always been easy and there have been some hardships and tears along the way. I am no stranger to crashing my motorcycle. My first crash was on the track, followed by several others in the dirt. My most embarrassing crash was in front of a group of students I was teaching, but that's riding for you: it can be random. Some of my friends have had much more serious crashes and they recovered. I am lucky that I have not had a close friend die while riding. I know it happens, and I see it far too often. Is the risk worth it? I often am asked and often ask myself that question. Absolutely. As an anonymous person once said, "Adventure may hurt you, but monotony will kill you."

I hope you see by now that two wheels really do move the soul, as well as the body. Your motorcycle journey may just have started, but I hope you've got a taste for how very rewarding motorcycle riding can be. Over the years, at 1st Gear, I've taught thousands of students to ride a motorcycle. It never ceases to amaze me how quickly these beginners develop into capable riders. It's a reminder that irrespective of how difficult and scary something looks, with time, respect, a little bit of money, and discipline, it can be mastered. This is as true for motorcycles as it is for near everything else.

Thinking about learning, I hope this book has given you the answers you were looking for. Learning to ride is a skill and one you will not forget. If for some reason it's not the time for you to ride, motorcycling will always be there when you're ready. If you're already riding, keep the rubber side down, and send me your pictures and stories of the incredible motorcycling experiences you've had. I love seeing my students on their new rides and hearing about the adventures they've had.

Since this is my first adventure in writing a book, and I want this to be a great resource for potential new riders, please let me know if there's any way I can improve Your First Motorcycle. I'll be sure to include your suggestions in the second edition, or an upcoming article. Your reviews would also be gratefully received.

With immense gratitude, thank you!

LEE RIDEFAR
www.ridefar.ca
www.1stgear.ca
leeridefar@gmail.com

ACKNOWLEDGMENTS

I want to thank everyone I've ever ridden with. And that is a long list! Thank you for the trips we've taken, track days, the laughs (and tears) we've shared, and the experiences, which will last a lifetime. May we ride safe and have more rides like Wrong Way Down, ExplOregon, and the Epic Adventure ahead of us.

Lionel, where would I be had I not met you in 2004 before I even knew how to ride? You were the one who introduced me to riding, and now we run an incredible motorcycle school together. How that all happened is beyond me. It must be crazy universe stuff at work. Your approach to life and business has been great to learn from and be a part of. It was a giant leap to start 1st Gear, but, wow, did it work out well.

My staff at 1st Gear—Melanie, Raymond, Larissa, Nicola, Patrick, John, Bruce, Tony, Adam, Otto, and Jeremy—thank you for joining our ride and ensuring the students that come through our doors get the knowledge, experience, and laughs they'll need to ride their first motorcycles. Working in the motorcycle industry ironically means little to no riding. Your help allowed me to still go on inspiring rides and write this book. That's rare and I truly appreciate it.

1st Gear students: You chose my school over several other great schools in Vancouver. You wrote the reviews, told your friends and shared your stories. I could not have imagined or forecasted how big 1st Gear was going to be. Your trust in 1st Gear and me made this book possible. Sure, I can make money teaching people how to ride, but the wealth of all these new friendships far exceeds it.

To everyone at Lioncrest Publishing and Book in a Box: thank you. Tucker Max, you came up with a great idea and talked me through some key moments. Molly and Emma, you were great to work with and asked all the right questions a new rider would ask. There is no way I could have come up with this on my own.

This book is dedicated to my parents. You didn't have to worry about me growing up. I required just a little more attention than the cats we had. The real worry began when I told you I had learned to ride a motorcycle. You were not thrilled, but like good parents, you accepted it. I followed that up by leaving a perfectly good, stable career as a financial planner to open up a new business teaching people to ride motorcycles. I now send home dozens of fresh new riders every week to tell their parents and loved ones, they ride a motorcycle. Oops! Funny how that has happened. Still, it's all worked out well, and your quiet curiosity and support was noted and appreciated. I will continue to keep it interesting, and I promise I won't ride over 300km/h on my track days. I love you more than words and motorcycles can express.

ABOUT THE
AUTHOR

LEE HEAVER runs and owns 1st Gear Motorcycle Training in Vancouver, Canada. Lee is a motorcycle enthusiast who has been riding for more than a decade, cruising some of North America's most spectacular roads and racetracks on every sort of motorcycle available. His blog, www.ridefar.ca, is widely read for its tips, interviews, and accounts of Lee's adventures in motorcycling. This is his first book.